CW00650161

THE POWER OF NOTION AI

Guide for Streamlining Business Productivity and Efficiency

Oleksandr Tsyhlin,
Dmytro Tsyhlin

Copyright © 2023 Oleksandr Tsyhlin, Dmytro Tsyhlin

No part of this book may be reproduced, stored in a retrieval system, or transmitted in any form or by any means, electronic, mechanical, photocopying, recording, or otherwise, without the express written permission of the publisher.
The information in this book is given as it is, without any guarantee. While the author and publisher have taken all necessary precautions during the preparation of this work, neither of them will be liable for any loss or damage, either directly or indirectly, that may be caused by the information contained in this book.

The authors do not have any affiliation with Notion Labs Inc.

CONTENTS

ABOUT AUTHORS

Oleksandr Tsyhlin is the executive director of Freedom Prime UK (London), which the subsidiary of the international group Freedom Holding Corp. (FRHC). He actively implements Notion as project management and a corporate wiki in the companies of the group at the enterprise level. He has over 15 years' experience launching projects in various fields (IT, finance, manufacturing).

Member of the Notion Champions program and holder of the Notion Essentials Badge

Contacts: https://www.linkedin.com/in/alextsyglin

Dmytro Tsyhlin - is the owner of a business selling physical goods on Amazon, and a professional marketplace sales specialist. He uses the Notion tool to manage products and orders and collect data to get the maximum return from each transaction. With over 17 years of experience in selling goods on the marketplaces all over the word, he is an expert in his field.

INTRODUCTION

Notion, a popular productivity app with over 20 million users, launched a new tool called Notion AI in February 2023. This feature is now available to users worldwide.

Notion AI helps you work faster, think bigger, and augment your creativity right inside the functional workspace you're already familiar with. If your day-to-day involves reading documents, writing content, or taking notes, Notion AI can make you more efficient. There's no need to bounce between tools to improve writing or extract insights. Plus, you don't need to waste time on formatting, formalities, or straightforward text generation, helping you lean into the highest priority tasks in your day.

Primary tasks that Notion AI can perform (A-Z):

- Brainstorm ideas
- Change the tone of text
- Convert any text into bullet points
- Create any tables from texts
- Create new blog post
- Create a social media post
- Create a press release
- Explain any word, sentence
- or paragraph
- Find action items after meeting
- Fix spelling & grammar
- Improve existing text
- Make text longer / shorter
- Simplify language
- Summarize any texts

- Translate into 14 languages any text
- Write a creative story
- Write an essay

This book explains how Notion AI works and provides real-life examples of its implementation in business.

More ideas and use cases of how AI can do work more productive you can find in our community **AI-Powered Business**

Solutions: aipbs.net

CHAPTER 1. WHAT IS NOTION AND NOTION AI?

What is Notion

Notion is a powerful productivity tool that aims to be an all-in-one workspace for personal and professional use. It allows users to create and organize notes, tasks, projects, databases, and more in one place, with the ability to customize the layout and design to fit their unique needs.

In Notion, there are several key components that make it a great product and applicable to any area (project management, knowledge portals, CRM, finance tracking, etc.). Notion also supports collaboration, allowing multiple users to work on the same pages and databases in real-time.

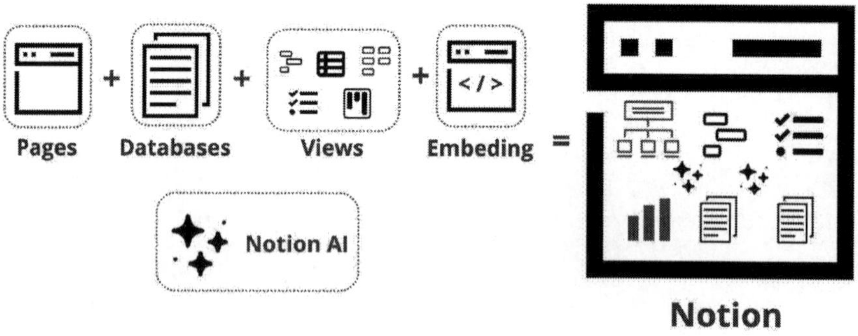

Notion killer features

Notion has an API and integrates with other popular tools and services, such as Google Drive, Trello, and Slack, making it a powerful hub for workflow management. Additionally, Notion offers an AI-powered feature called Notion AI, which can help automate tasks and suggest ways to optimize workflows. Notion has web app, Mac, Windows, iOS, and Android versions.

Users can use Notion for free, but with some limitations. For example, free users can only access the last 7 days of page history and can only invite up to 10 guests. Alternatively, users can purchase a paid plan and gain access to additional features that allow for more effective collaboration within a team.

If you are new to Notion, we would appreciate it if you used our affiliate link to register: https://affiliate.notion.so/tsyhlin-notionai

What is Notion AI? Is it the same as ChatGPT?

Notion AI is an AI module for Notion that helps you work faster, think bigger, and augment your creativity right inside the functional workspace you're already familiar with.

Notion AI uses the OpenAI ChatGPT model. This is referenced in their Third-Party Provider Policies.

> ***Third-Party Provider Policies*** *If you choose to use the Notion AI feature(s), you may not use the Notion AI features in a manner that violates any OpenAI Policy, including their Content Policy; Sharing and Publication Policy; and Community Guidelines.*

Source: https://www.notion.so/Notion-AI-Supplementary-Terms-fa9034c8b5a04818a6baf3eac2adddbb

However, when we asked Notion support which of the GPT models Notion uses in Notion AI (GPT-3 or GPT-4) they did not provide a direct answer.

They said that since the world of AI is rapidly evolving and Notion AI is still in its early stages, they are continuously evaluating numerous AI models to see which are best suited to Notion's unique interface.

It looks like both ChatGPT and Notion AI offer AI-powered solutions to make things easier. However, they serve different purposes. ChatGPT is great for generating human-like text responses to user input, making it a powerful tool for automating customer service and content creation. Meanwhile, Notion AI is geared towards simplifying and streamlining workflows by automating repetitive tasks and offering suggestions and templates to users.

ChatGPT's strength is in its ability to understand and respond to natural language, making it perfect for personalized and contextually appropriate responses. This is great for companies looking to automate their customer service and support operations, as well as content creators looking to generate high-quality and engaging content more efficiently.

Notion AI, on the other hand, is more focused on making workflows simpler and more efficient by offering suggestions and automating repetitive tasks. It has a variety of features, including completion suggestions, formatting options, and pre-made templates, making it a versatile tool for individuals and teams looking to boost productivity and efficiency.

How accurate are Notion AI's responses?

Notion AI is super effective for streamlining your workflows, like summarizing meeting notes and brainstorming to get you started. But Notion recommends that you always double-check the accuracy of content generated by Notion AI before relying on it for critical content.

Here is a text from the official Notion web-site:

Notion does not guarantee the accuracy of any information obtained through Notion AI, and any material or data obtained through the use of any Notion AI feature is done at your own risk. You should fact-check any factual assertions before relying on them, as outputs that appear accurate due to their specificity may still contain inaccuracies.

Notion AI cannot dynamically retrieve information and may not account for events or changes to underlying facts occurring after the AI model was trained (the date of the last training Notion AI is not disclosed by Notion)

Source:https://www.notion.so/Notion-AI-Supplementary-Terms-fa9034c8b5a04818a6baf3eac2adddbb

Does Notion use my data to train Notion AI?

Notion does not use your customer data to teach the robots that power the Notion AI. Additionally, using the Notion AI does not grant Notion the right to use your data.

Your data is still encrypted and private following Notion's standard data protection practices.

However, machine-learning robots and AI can improve over time. Notion may use data from your use of Notion AI to enhance the intelligence of the robots. This can occur when you provide feedback by indicating whether you like or dislike the output, or when you allow Notion to utilize your data.

To do this - click to the Like button after AI output (1) and then press Share this AI session with Notion (2)

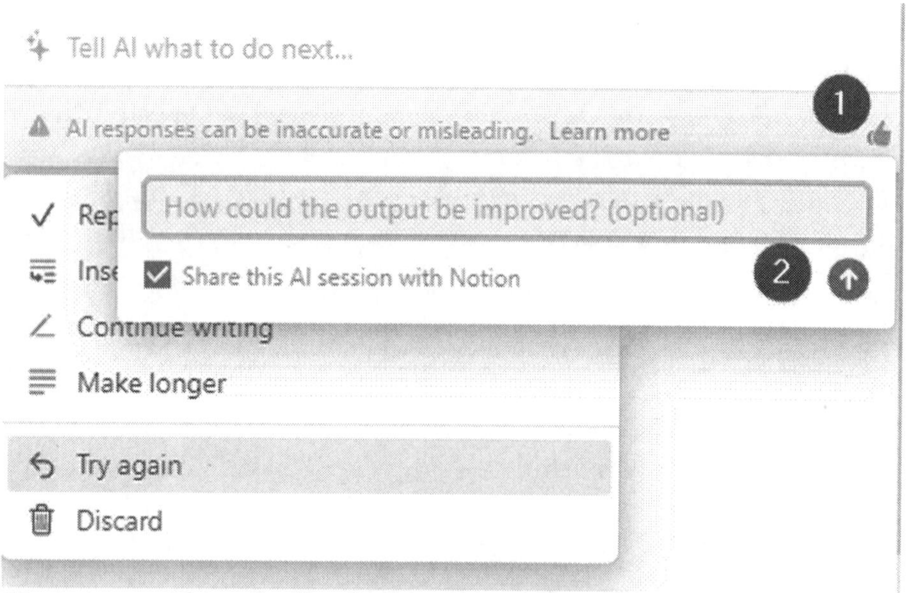

How you can share feedback about AI quality with Notion

Source: https://www.notion.so/Notion-AI-Supplementary-Terms-fa9034c8b5a04818a6baf3eac2adddbb

Also, Notion AI only accesses content from the page where you're using it.

Does Notion own my data that I created by Notion AI?

You own all the customer data, and that includes all intellectual property rights in it. But just because you give that data to Notion doesn't mean that they suddenly own it. Notion has your permission to use your stuff in specific ways. Notion can host, store, transfer, display, perform, reproduce, modify, create derivative works of, and distribute customer data.

Source: **Master Subscription Agreement,** Part 3. **Ownership of Intellectual Property; License Grant**

https://www.notion.so/Master-Subscription-Agreement-4e1c5dd3e3de45dfa4a8ed60f1a43da0

CHAPTER 2. HOW TO USE NOTION AI

Setting up Notion and Notion AI

After you register in Notion (we would appreciate it if you use our affiliate link to register): https://notion.grsm.io/tsyhlin

1. On the 1st screen you need to enter your email, and code, that you'll receive on this email

2. On the second screen, enter your name (if you register as a member of a big team, we recommend using your full name), password, and password; you can also add your photo.

3. On the next screen - choose how you are planning to use Notion. If you want to try it for yourself - choose "For personal use", if you want to use Notion in your Team - choose "For my team". If you are taught or student - choose "For school"

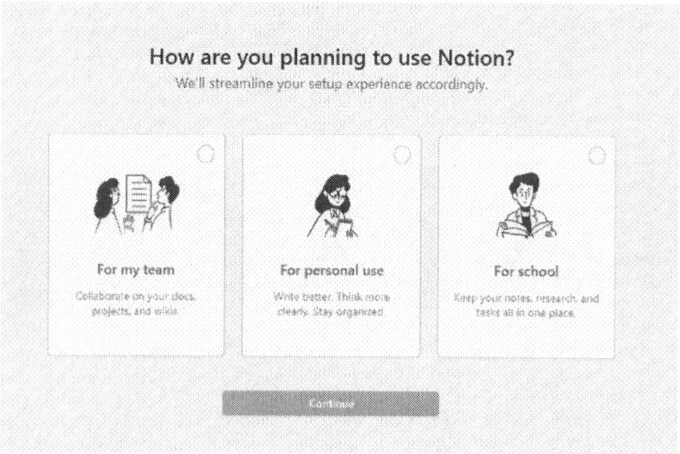

4. On the next screen, fill out several questions about your work and your roles.

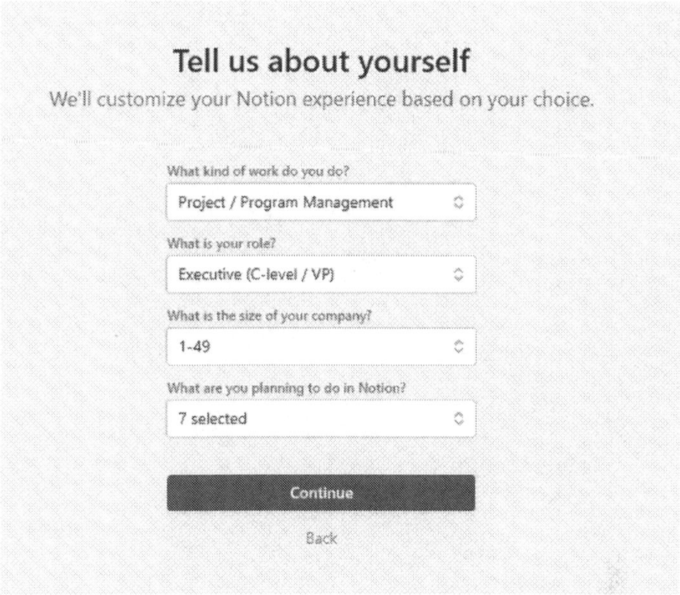

5. Create a Team workspace (place where you'll store all data with your team) by choosing icon for your workspace (your can add your custom icon if you want)

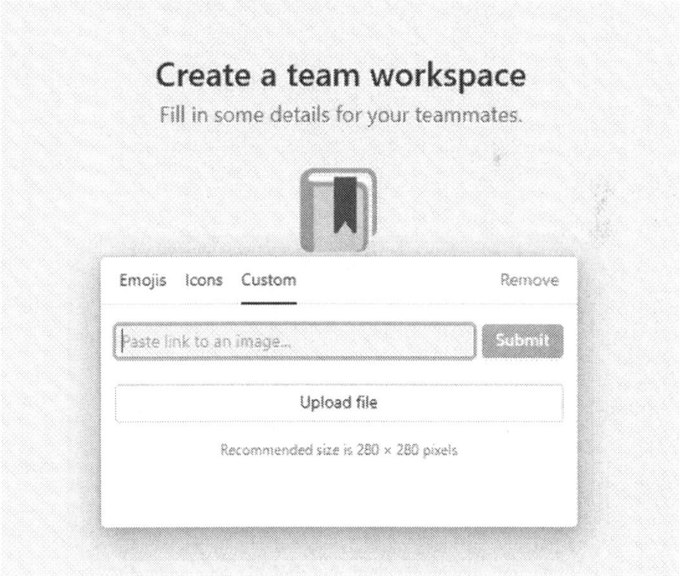

and workspace name

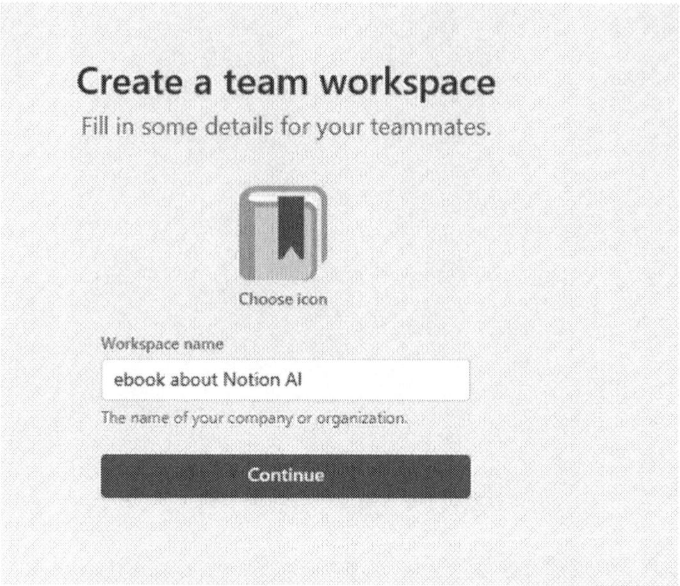

6. On the next screen, you can invite your colleagues to your workspace by email or share the link with them so they can register for your team's workspace.

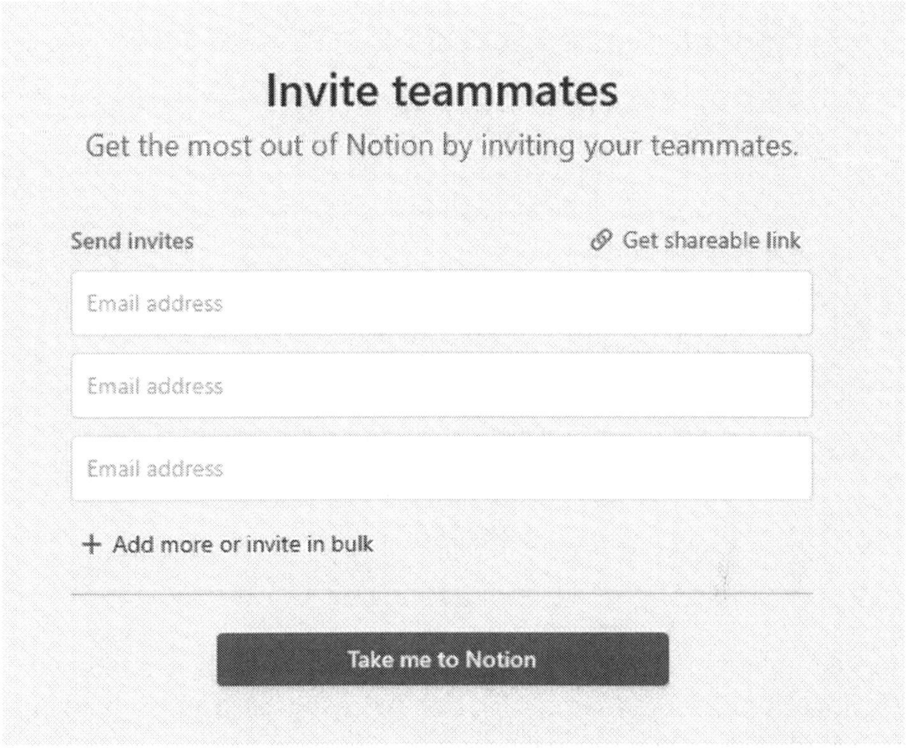

If you have many colleagues, use the bulk feature to add them.

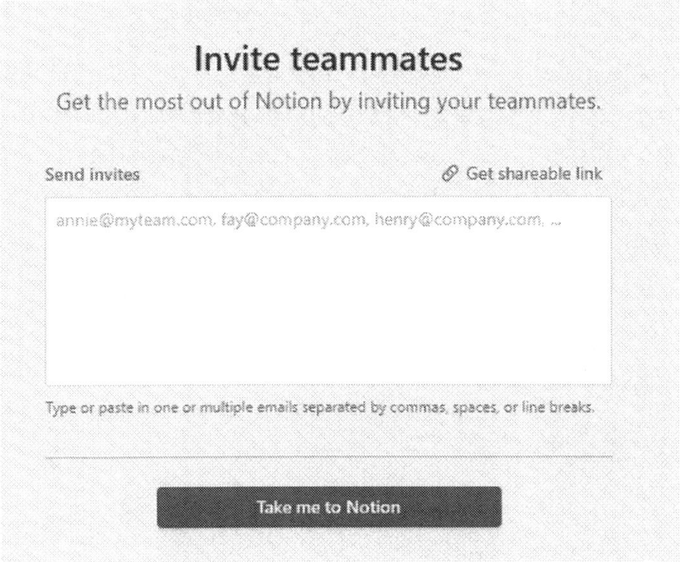

Once you are finished, click the button "Take me to Notion."

On the next screen, you will see the Notion workspace, which consists of the following main sections:

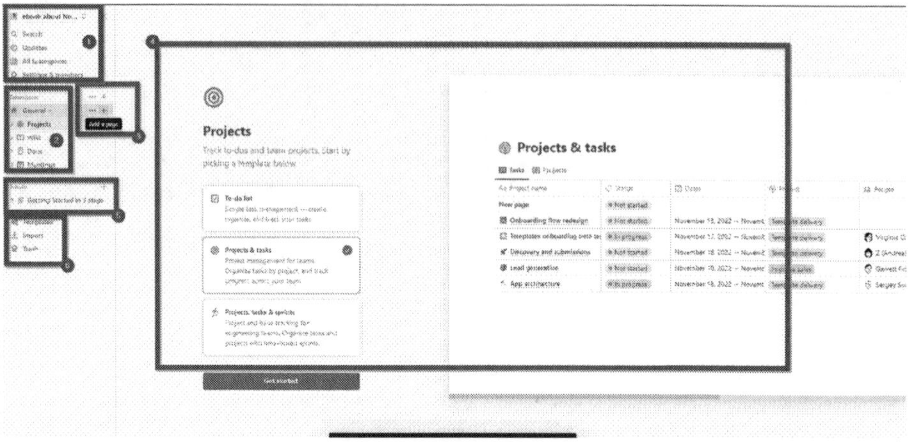

1. System Area: Here you can see the Search Area, Updates and Notifications, and a List of all your Teamspaces, and the Settings and Members area.

In settings & members menu we can change our tariff and buy Notion AI feature

2. Workspace area: here you can find all the pages and documents related to your workspace. After you log in to Notion for the first time, it will offer you several standard templates for different tasks (Projects, Wiki, Docs, Meetings).

You can delete them by clicking on the three dots next to the name and selecting "Delete" and creating your own page.

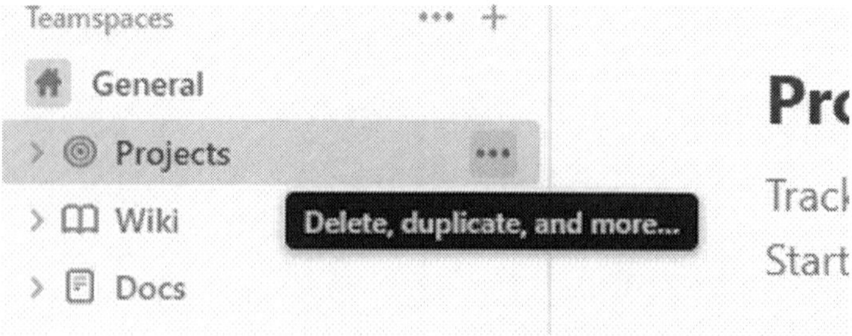

3. Create your own page by clicking on the "+" icon next to the Teamspace name.

You can read more about what Teamspaces are here: https://www.notion.so/help/guides/teamspaces-give-teams-home-for-important-work

4. The main workspace for working within the page you have selected is located on the right side.

The page itself is located in the left menu (1), and on the right, you will see the page title (2) and below it, the workspace with the content (3).

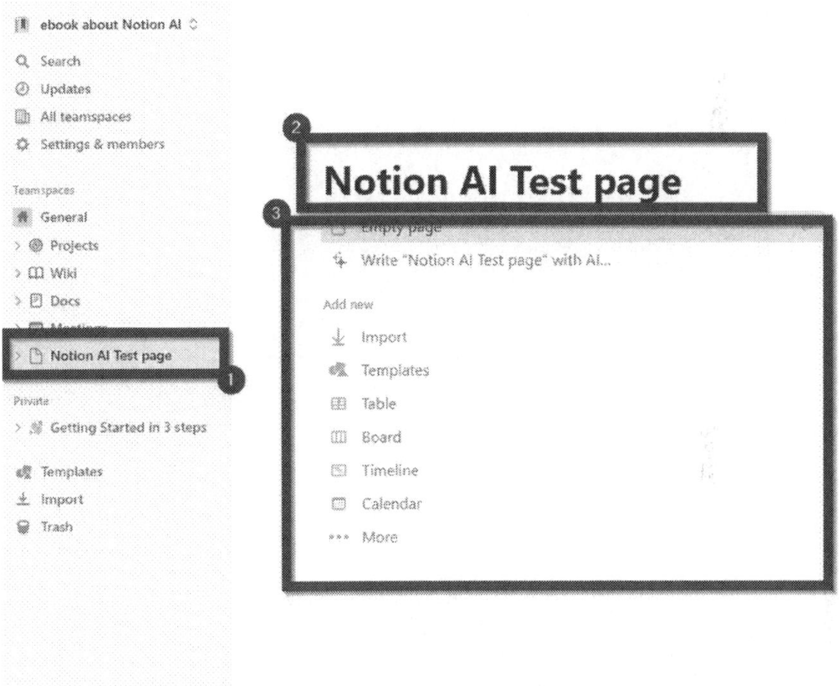

5. There is also an area for Private Pages, which are pages that only you have access to.

6. At the bottom left, there are links to Notion's Page Templates, a button to import your data into Notion, and a trash can where all the pages you delete go.

You can read more about importing data into Notion here: https://www.notion.so/help/import-data-into-notion

Here's how to find a page in the trash: https://www.notion.so/help/duplicate-delete-and-restore-content

5 ways how to turn on Notion AI

Way 1. On a blank page, click on a button. Start writing with AI

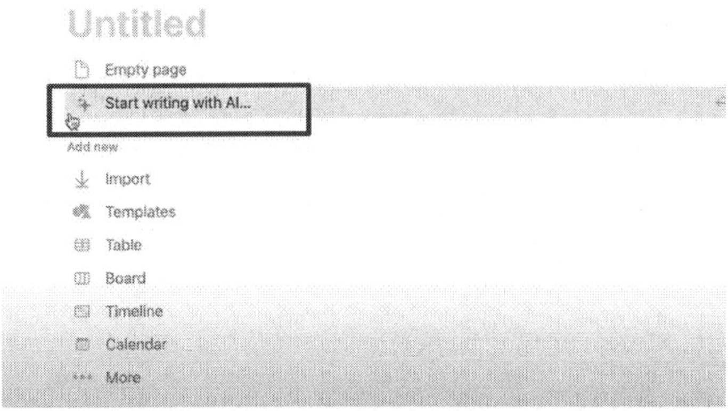

Way 2. Press Space in any blank row in any page

and you'll see Notion AI dialog

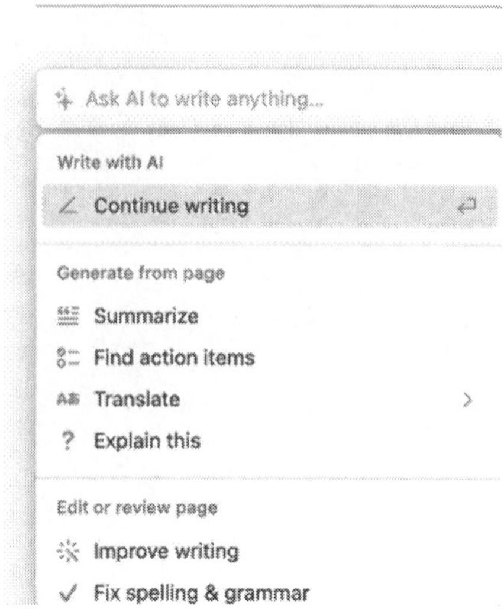

Way 3. Type the command /ai in any Notion page

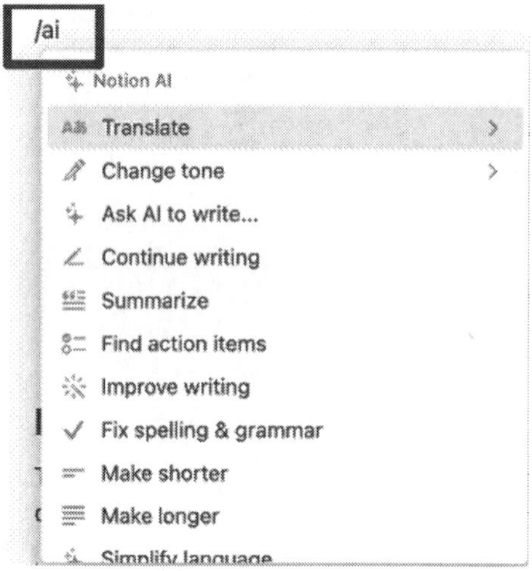

Way 4. Use AI shortcut

Use shortcut CTRL+J (CMD+J for mac)

Way 5. Choose the text you want to work with AI and click Ask AI

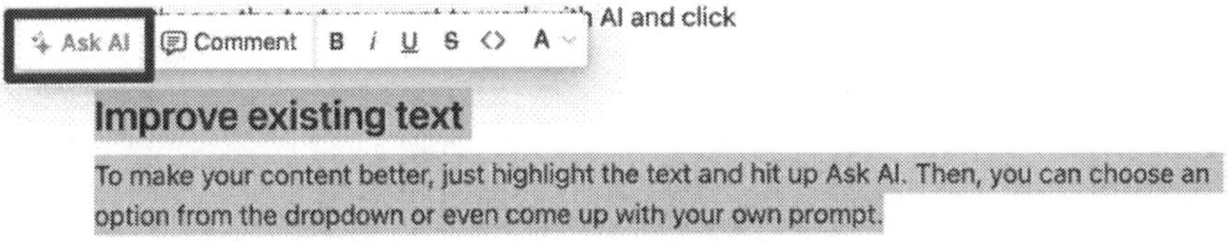
AI and click
Ask AI
Comment
Improve existing text
To make your content better, just highlight the text and hit up Ask AI. Then, you can choose an option from the dropdown or even come up with your own prompt.

How to buy subscription to Notion AI

Before we start using Notion AI regularly, we will need to purchase a subscription, as the free plan only includes 20 AI requests.

Notion AI is available as an add-on to all Notion plans, including Free Plans, for $10 per member, per month. A 20% discount is available to Plus, Business, and Enterprise customers with annual billing.

Just a heads up: if you're an annual customer, you won't be able to snag Notion AI with monthly billing. And if you're on the free plan or a monthly customer, you won't be able to grab Notion AI with annual billing either.

To do this, go to the Settings section.

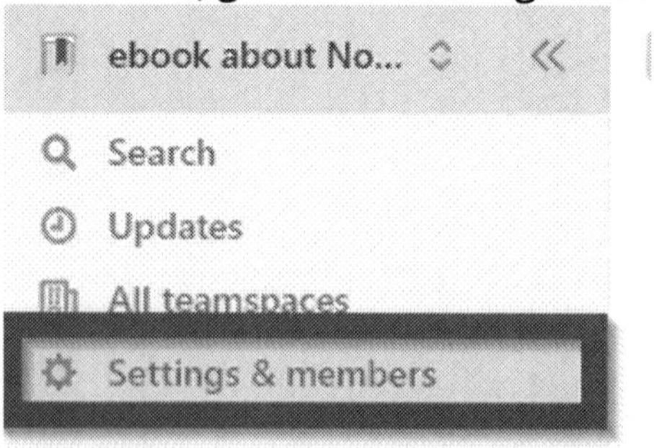

Next, go to the Upgrade tab, and here you will see how many free AI requests you have left. To activate your subscription, click "Add to plan."

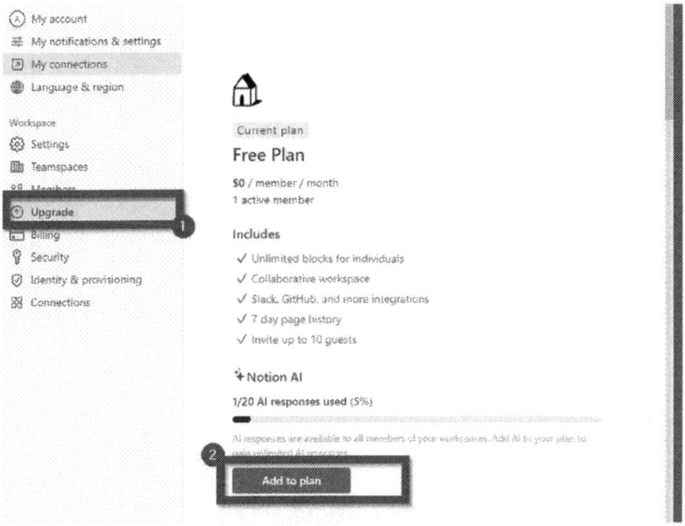

So, if you decide to add Notion AI to your already-paid plan, you'll only have to pay for the time you have left in your current billing cycle. Then, once your next billing date rolls around, the AI add-on charge will tag along with your regular billing schedule.

So, if you're a free user and you sign up for Notion AI, your billing cycle starts on the same day. And every month from then on, you'll be charged on that same day. Easy peasy!

On the next screen, enter your payment details and click "Upgrade now."

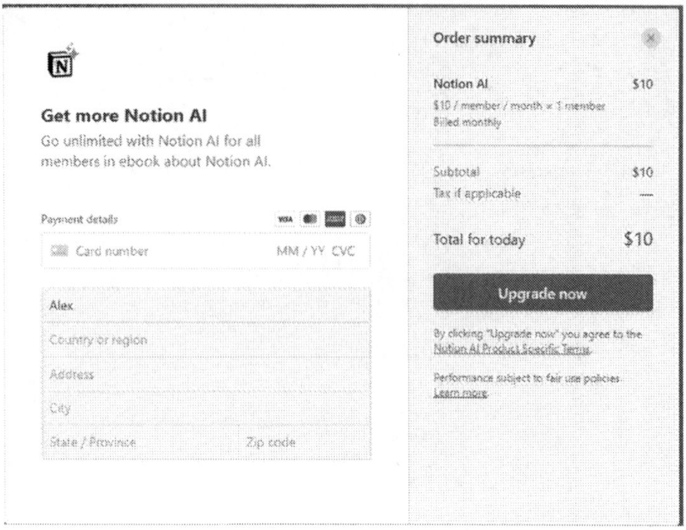

Now you a ready to active day to day work with Notion AI

Sharing of Notion AI with team members and guests

Is it possible to buy Notion AI for only some of my team, without buying for the whole workspace?

Unfortunately, you can't just get it for a part of your workspace right now.

But, if you do go ahead and get AI for your workspace, everybody in that workspace can use it. That means everybody, from the owners to the members, can use those sweet AI features.

Can guests use Notion AI?

Guests will not be able to use AI features in your workspace.

More Q&A about pricing Notion AI you can find here: https://www.notion.so/help/ai-pricing-and-usage

How to cancel Notion AI subscription

1 - Click on Settings & members in your sidebar

2 - Click on Upgrade or Billing int the sidebar

3 - if you finally decided to stop using this service - click Remove from plan

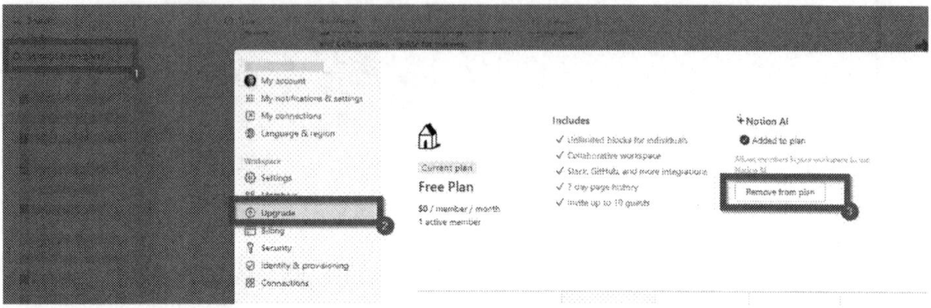

So, here's the deal: if you're on the Free Plan and you decide to get rid of Notion AI, you'll still have it for the rest of this billing cycle. But come the next cycle, you won't be able to use it anymore.

And, if you're on a Paid Plan and decide to cancel subscription to Notion AI, it'll be gone right away. Plus, any time you didn't use will be credited back to your account.

Examples of the use of Notion AI

So, Notion AI is like your personal text buddy who gives you answers based on what you're asking and the page you're on. Here are the ways to get Notion AI on your screen, depending on your needs at the moment.

Change tone of text

Notion AI can replace complex texts with simpler words and describe them in different styles.

To do this, just highlight the text in (1) and hit up Ask AI. Then, you can choose the option Change tone from the drop-down menu (2). And press Friendly

Below is an example of describing Newton's First Law using simple words.

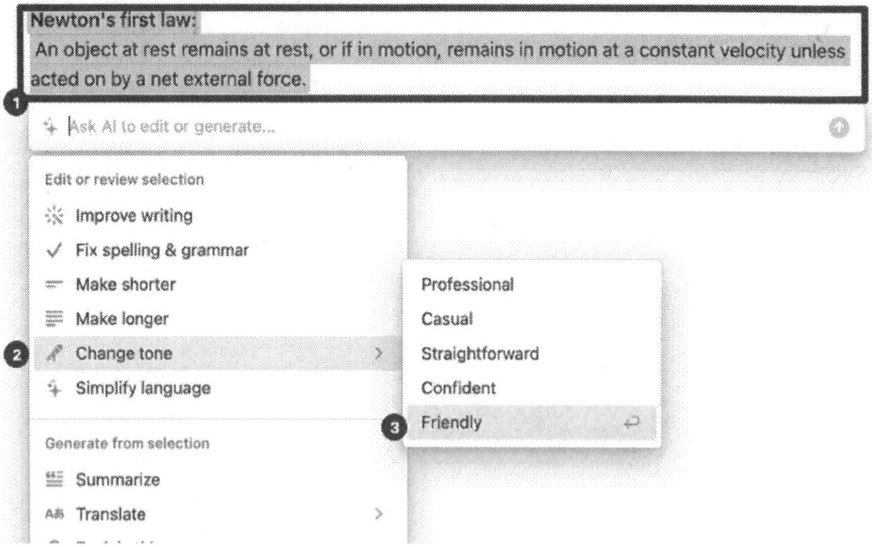

Results:

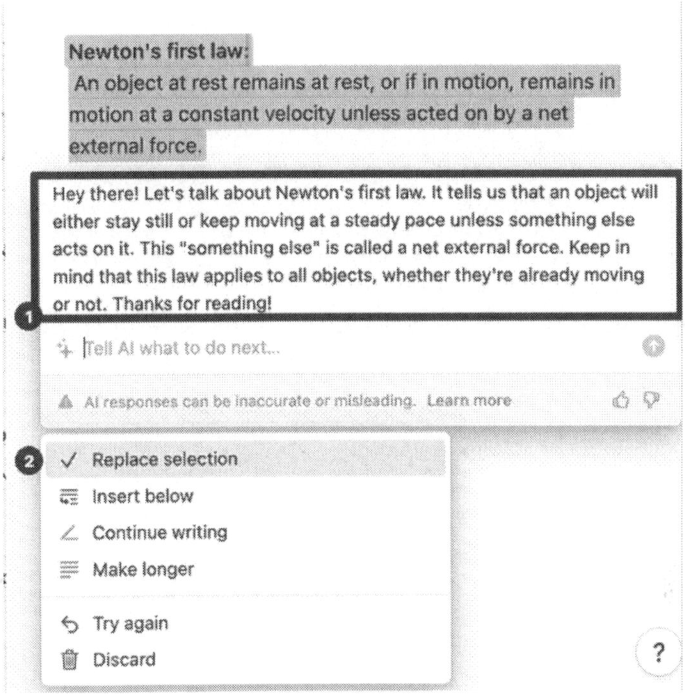

*Below one more example how Notion simplify text from the Limited Liability Company Act:***

"Limited liability company agreement" means any agreement (whether referred to as a limited liability company agreement, an operating agreement, or otherwise), written, oral, or implied, of the member or members as to the affairs of a limited liability company and the conduct of its business. A member or manager of a limited liability company or an assignee of a limited liability company's interest is bound by the limited liability company agreement whether the member, manager, or assignee executes the limited liability company agreement or not.

Output from Notion AI:

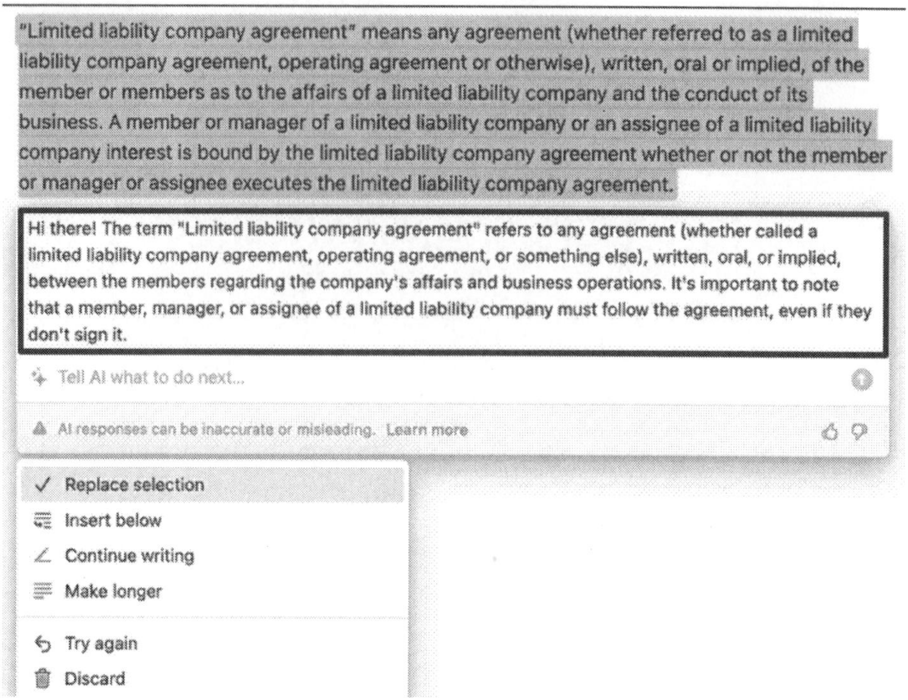

You can also to make text more simple with command simplify language and press Enter

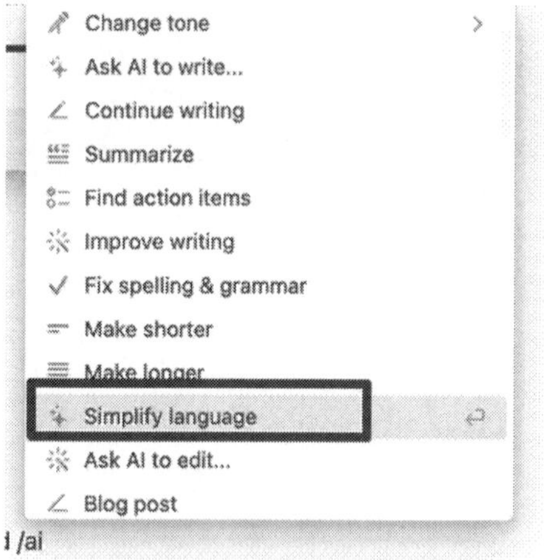

Just highlight the text you want to simplify and use this command

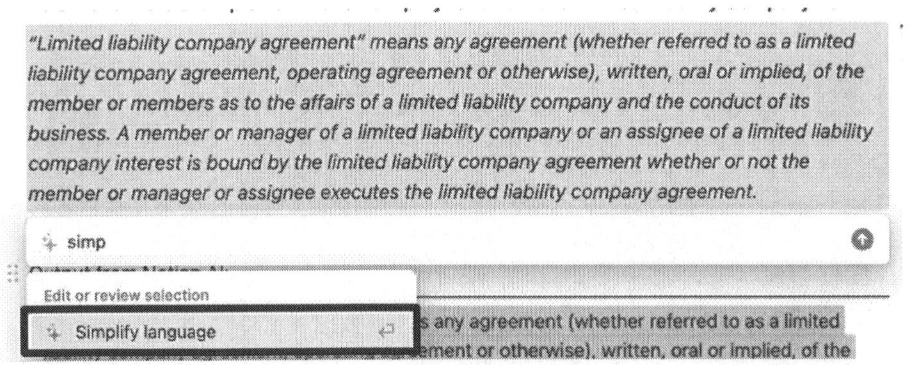
"Limited liability company agreement" means any agreement (whether referred to as a limited liability company agreement, operating agreement or otherwise), written, oral or implied, of the member or members as to the affairs of a limited liability company and the conduct of its business. A member or manager of a limited liability company or an assignee of a limited liability company interest is bound by the limited liability company agreement whether or not the member or manager or assignee executes the limited liability company agreement.
simp
Edit or review selection
Simplify language
any agreement (whether referred to as a limited
ement or otherwise), written, oral or implied, of the

Convert into bullet points

Use prompt convert into bullet points **to convert text into bullet points**

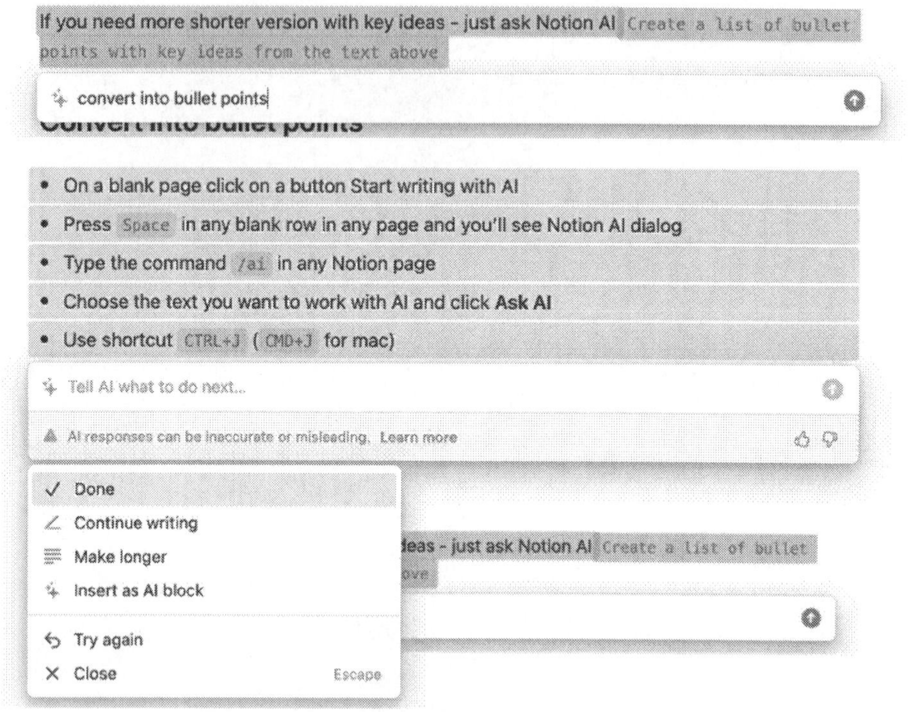

Create a tables

Any kind data in table view

Asking Notion AI to write something in a table format with command /ai → in a table ...

important to specify with a comma - column

Example of input:

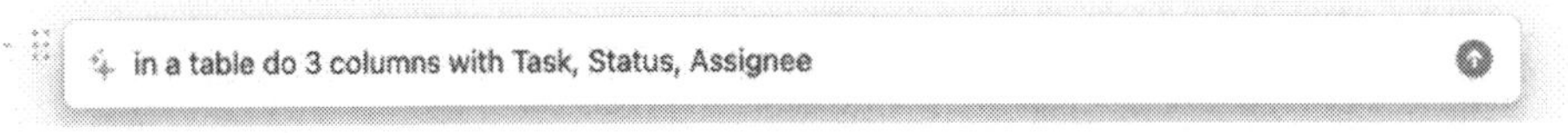

Example of output:

After you see a table - you can convert it to database

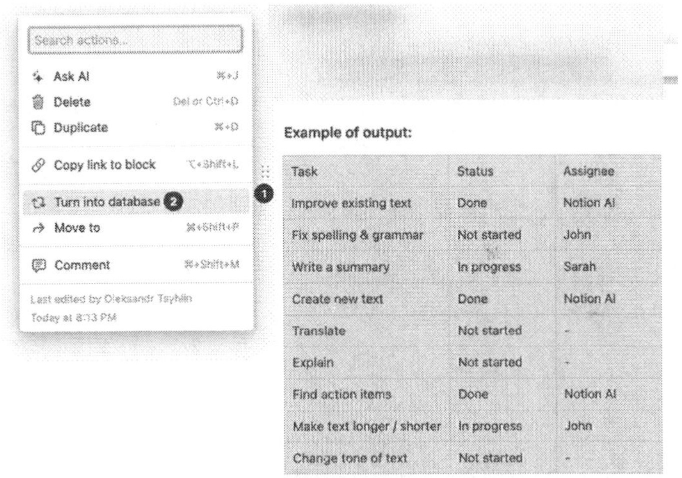

Task	Status	Assignee
Improve existing text	Done	Notion AI
Fix spelling & grammar	Not started	John
Write a summary	In progress	Sarah
Create new text	Done	Notion AI
Translate	Not started	-
Explain	Not started	-
Find action items	Done	Notion AI
Make text longer / shorter	In progress	John
Change tone of text	Not started	-

Results after converting to a database:

Table

Filter Sort New

Untitled

Title	Status	Assignee
Improve existing text	Done	Notion AI
Fix spelling & grammar	Not started	John
Write a summary	In progress	Sarah
Create new text	Done	Notion AI
Translate	Not started	-
Explain	Not started	-
Find action items	Done	Notion AI
Make text longer / shorter	In progress	John
Change tone of text	Not started	-

+ New

Comparison tables

Asking Notion AI to compare something in a table view will generate a comparison analysis table.

To activate it, type **/AI** to view AI blocks or press Space on the blank row, and ask Notion AI to Create a comparison table of.... .

example of a comparison table created by Notion AI about **volleyball** and **beach volleyball,** where the prompt was Create a comparison table between volleyball and beach volleyball (1) and below prompt you see the output from Notion AI (2) - it creating this table and filling it in real time

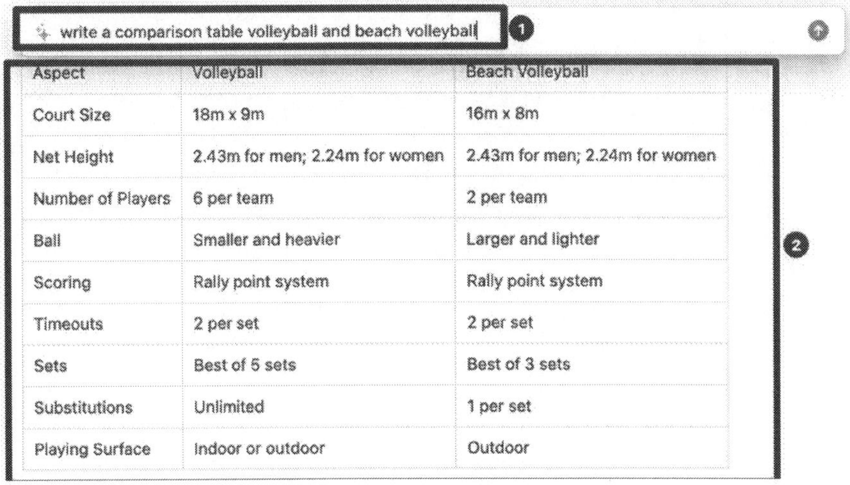

Aspect	Volleyball	Beach Volleyball
Court Size	18m x 9m	16m x 8m
Net Height	2.43m for men; 2.24m for women	2.43m for men; 2.24m for women
Number of Players	6 per team	2 per team
Ball	Smaller and heavier	Larger and lighter
Scoring	Rally point system	Rally point system
Timeouts	2 per set	2 per set
Sets	Best of 5 sets	Best of 3 sets
Substitutions	Unlimited	1 per set
Playing Surface	Indoor or outdoor	Outdoor

Create new blog post

Type **/AI** to view AI blocks, or press Space on the blank row, and ask Notion AI to write anything for you in different formats:

- Brainstorm ideas
- Blog post
- Outline
- Social media post
- Press release
- Creative story
- Essay

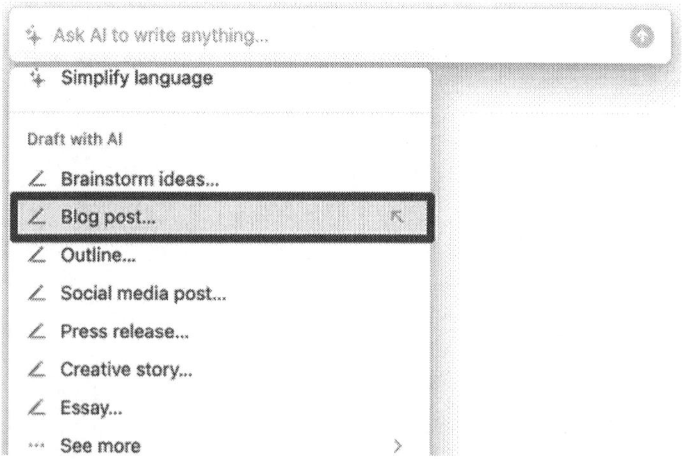

If you like the text Notion AI generated and you want to get more text, just highlight the text and click the button Continue writing

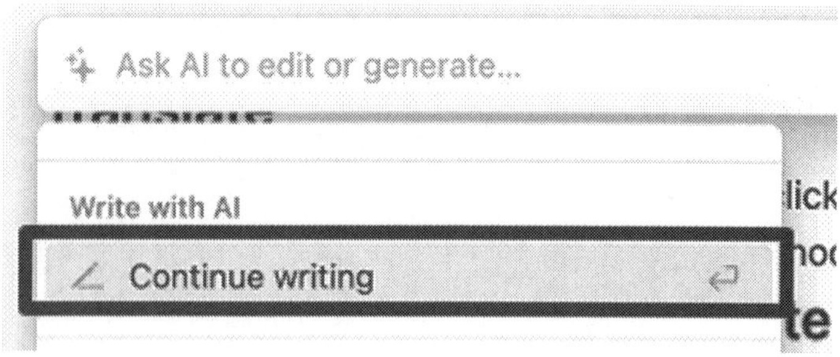

Create a post from outline

Type /AI to view AI blocks or press Space on the blank row, and ask Notion AI to write Outline:

On the next screen, write your request to Notion AI, and it will create an outline according to your request.

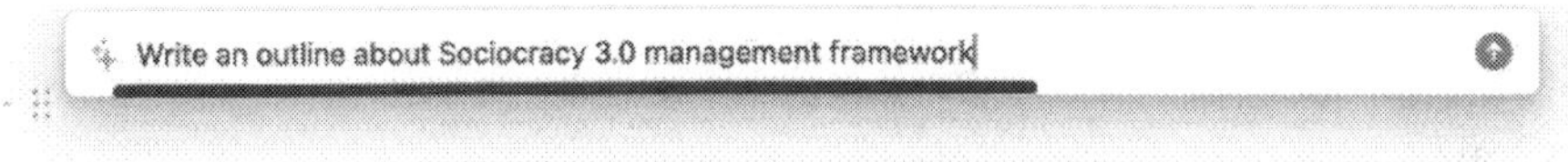

Explain

Notion AI can explain any text that you copied in Notion. To activite it type /AI to view AI blocks or press Space on the blank row, and ask Notion AI to Explain.

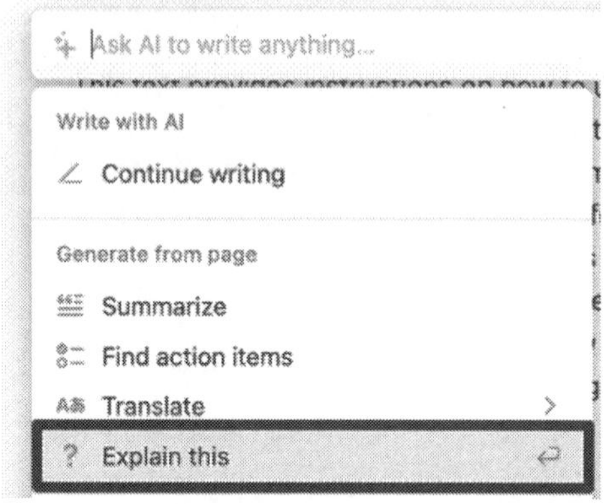

Example of explanation on this page, generated by Notion AI:

This text provides instructions on how to use Notion AI, a feature of the Notion productivity application. Notion AI can help improve existing text, generate summaries, create new text, and translate content. To use these features, users can highlight text and click "Ask AI" to access a drop-down menu of options. Users can also type "/AI" to view AI blocks or press space on a blank row to create new text. Notion AI can also be used to translate text by selecting the desired text and language from the dropdown menu.

You can also ask to explain a specific word; just highlight the word you want to be explained (1) click Ask AI (or CTRL/CMD + J) and click Explain this (2)

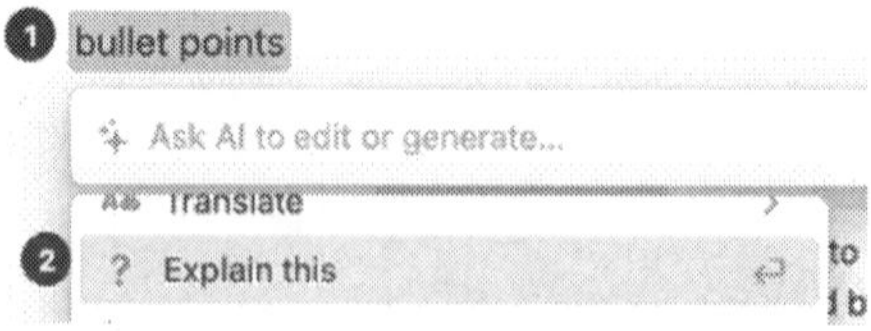

Example of explanation word bullet points by Notion AI:

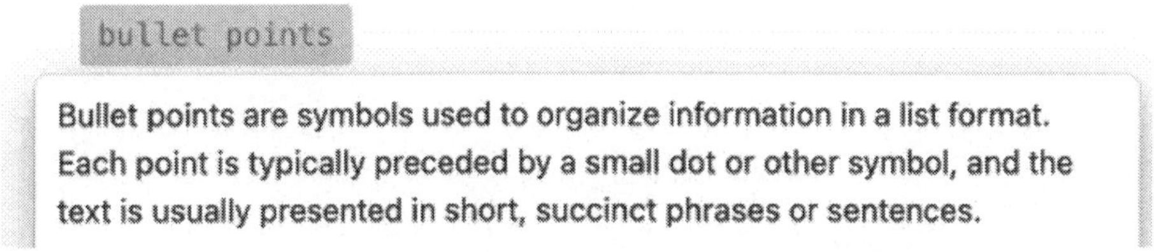
bullet points
Bullet points are symbols used to organize information in a list format. Each point is typically preceded by a small dot or other symbol, and the text is usually presented in short, succinct phrases or sentences.

Find action items

To find out what needs to be done in the content, just highlight paragraph (1) and hit up Ask AI. Then, you can choose an option called Find action items from the drop-down menu (2).

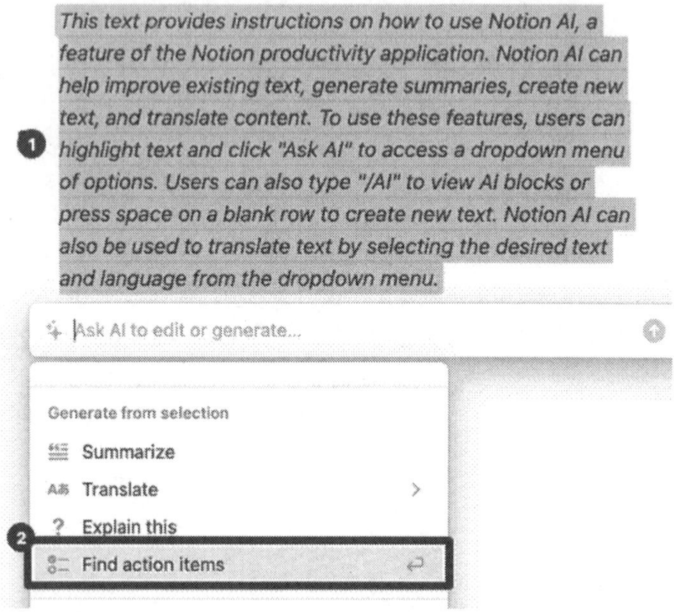

This is how Notion AI extracts action items from text. If you find it useful, click Insert below, and it will be pasted under the highlighted text.

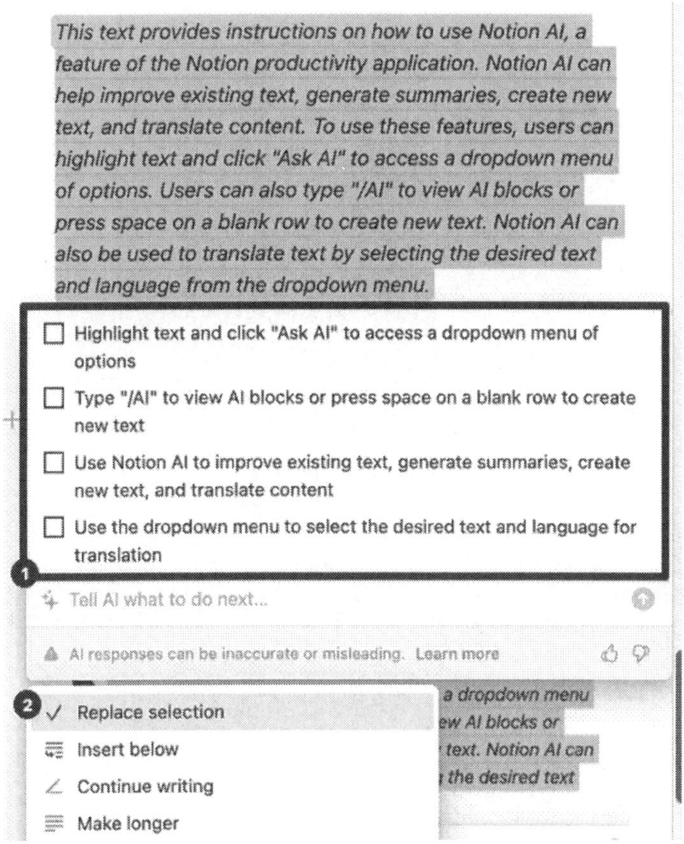
This text provides instructions on how to use Notion AI, a feature of the Notion productivity application. Notion AI can help improve existing text, generate summaries, create new text, and translate content. To use these features, users can highlight text and click "Ask AI" to access a dropdown menu of options. Users can also type "/AI" to view AI blocks or press space on a blank row to create new text. Notion AI can also be used to translate text by selecting the desired text and language from the dropdown menu.
Highlight text and click "Ask AI" to access a dropdown menu of options
Type "/AI" to view AI blocks or press space on a blank row to create new text
Use Notion AI to improve existing text, generate summaries, create new text, and translate content
Use the dropdown menu to select the desired text and language for translation
1
Tell AI what to do next...
AI responses can be inaccurate or misleading. Learn more
2
Replace selection
Insert below
Continue writing
Make longer

Fix spelling & grammar

To make your content better, just highlight the text and hit up Ask AI. Then, you can choose an option from the dropdown Fix spelling & grammar

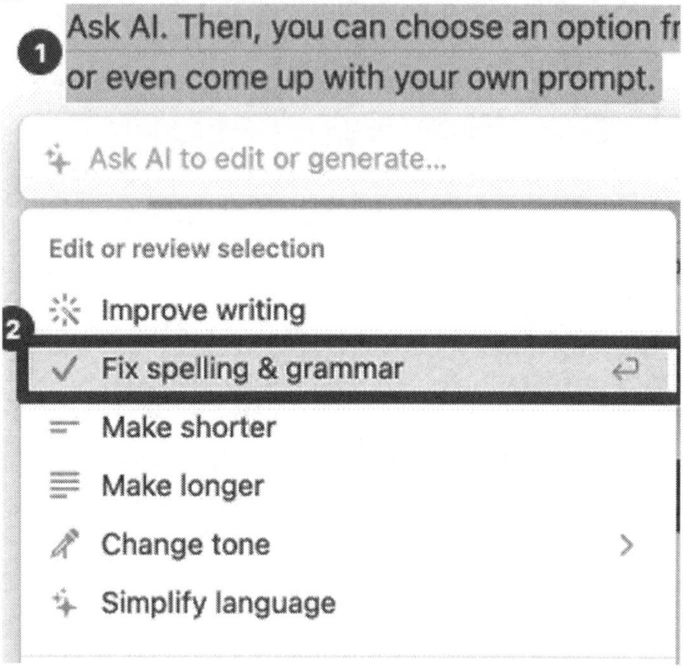

Improve existing text

To make your content better, just highlight the text and hit up Ask AI. Then, you can choose an option from the dropdown or even come up with your own prompt.

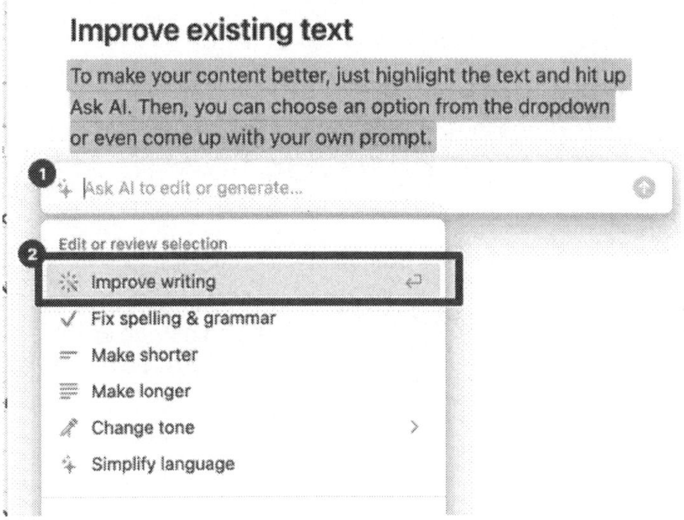

Make text longer / shorter

If you need to generate more content from this page, just highlight the text in (1) and hit up Ask AI. Then, you can choose the option Make longer from the drop-down menu (2).

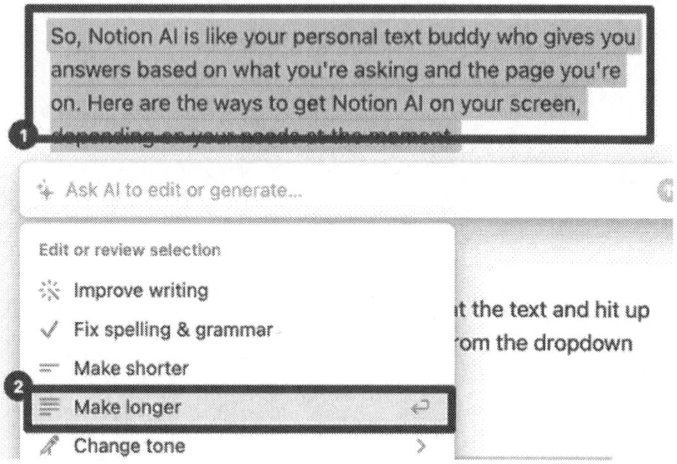
So, Notion AI is like your personal text buddy who gives you
answers based on what you're asking and the page you're
on. Here are the ways to get Notion AI on your screen,
1
Ask AI to edit or generate...
Edit or review selection
Improve writing
Fix spelling & grammar
Make shorter
2
Make longer
Change tone
the text and hit up
the dropdown

Below is an example of how Notion AI generated three paragraphs of text from one paragraph on the topic of what Notion AI is and how it can be useful (1). If you like it, click Replace selection (2), and it will be pasted instead of the highlighted text.

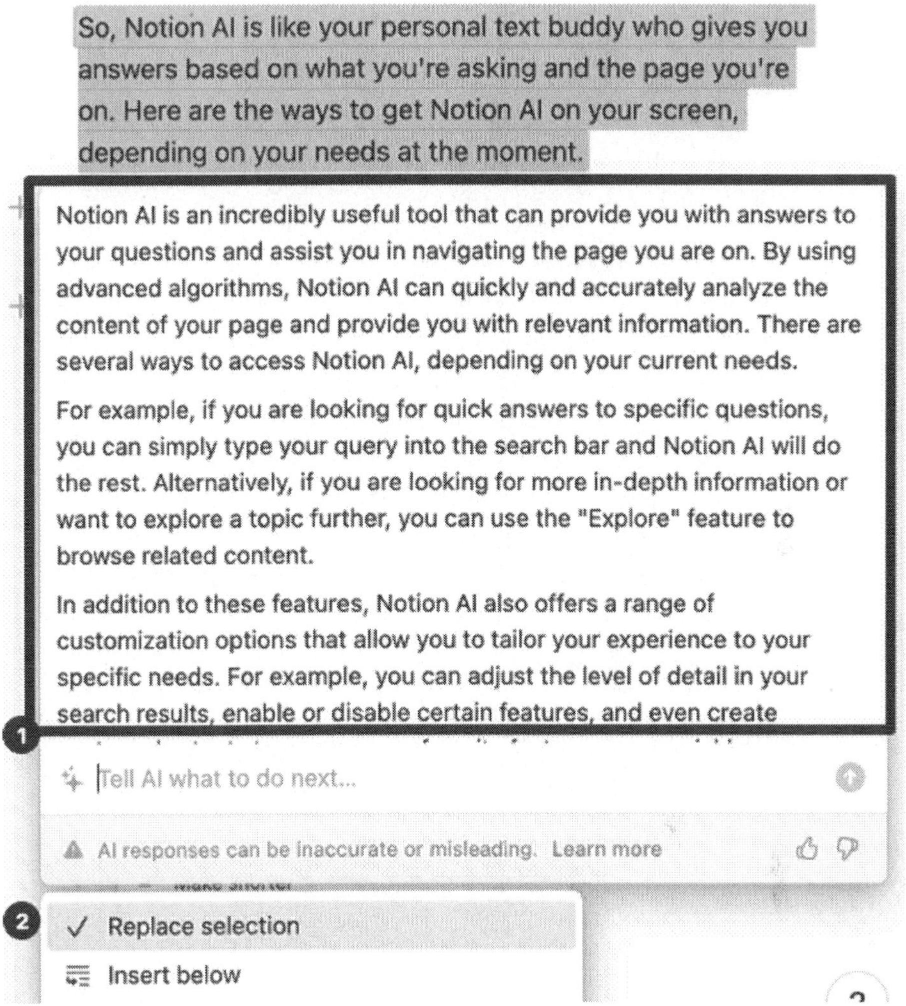
So, Notion AI is like your personal text buddy who gives you answers based on what you're asking and the page you're on. Here are the ways to get Notion AI on your screen, depending on your needs at the moment.
Notion AI is an incredibly useful tool that can provide you with answers to your questions and assist you in navigating the page you are on. By using advanced algorithms, Notion AI can quickly and accurately analyze the content of your page and provide you with relevant information. There are several ways to access Notion AI, depending on your current needs.
For example, if you are looking for quick answers to specific questions, you can simply type your query into the search bar and Notion AI will do the rest. Alternatively, if you are looking for more in-depth information or want to explore a topic further, you can use the "Explore" feature to browse related content.
In addition to these features, Notion AI also offers a range of customization options that allow you to tailor your experience to your specific needs. For example, you can adjust the level of detail in your search results, enable or disable certain features, and even create
1
Tell AI what to do next...
AI responses can be inaccurate or misleading. Learn more
2
Replace selection
Insert below

Pros and Cons block by Notion AI

Notion AI can write a pros and cons list; to do this, just highlight the text (1) and hit up Ask AI. Then, start typing phrase Pros and cons list and choose it

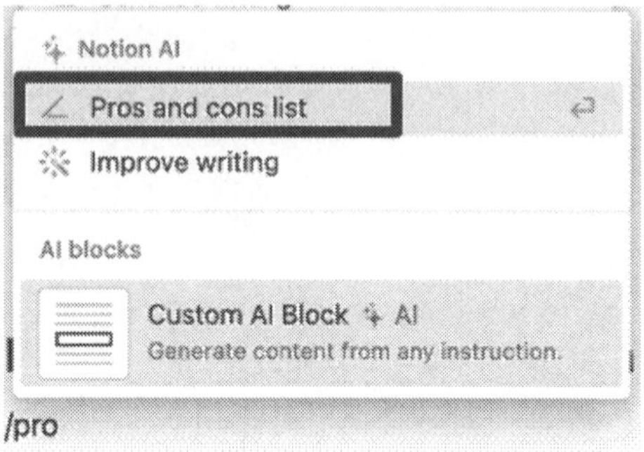

You can write Pros and Cons about any topic you want

Or you can write Pros and Cons about text that you wrote

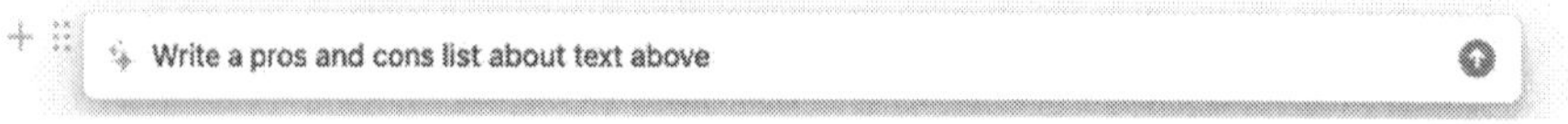

Example of Pros and Cons about this charter Notion AI

Pros

- Provides detailed instructions on how to use Notion AI to improve, summarize, and translate text.
- Explains how to use Notion AI to create new blog posts, outlines, and social media posts.
- Offers various ways to activate Notion AI on the page, including using a shortcut key or typing a command.
- Includes screenshots and examples to help users understand each feature.
- Can generate a pros and cons list using the "Ask AI" feature.

Cons

- Assumes users have a basic understanding of Notion and its features.
- Does not cover all of the features and capabilities of Notion AI.
- Some of the prompts for Notion AI can be difficult to remember or find.
- Notion AI may not always provide the desired output or may require additional editing to make the content usable.
- Not all users may find the AI-generated content helpful or relevant to their needs.

Translate

To translate the content, highlight the text and click "Ask AI" (1). Then, select the text you want to translate (2) from the drop-down menu, and choose the language you want to translate into (3).

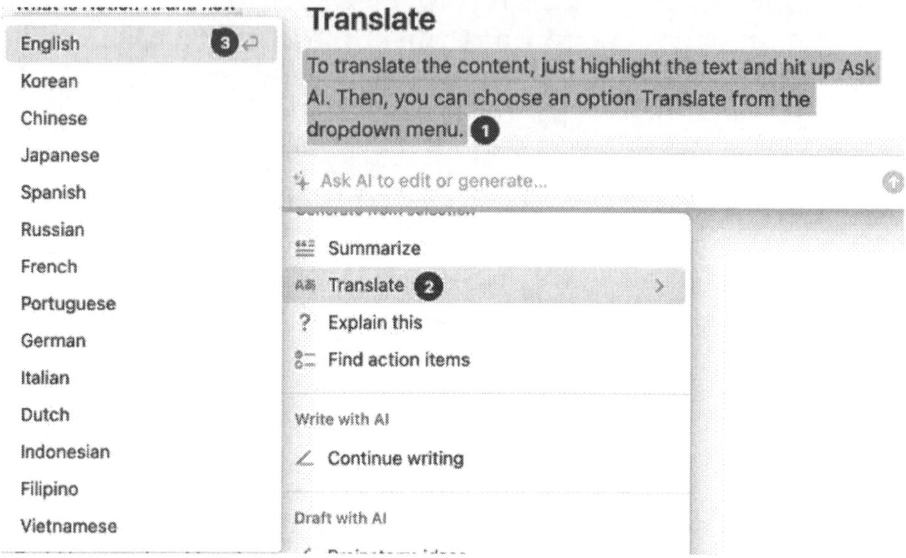

Write a story

Notion AI can write creative stories, to do this start AI with Space button in any blank page. Then, start typing Story

Enter prompt for your story

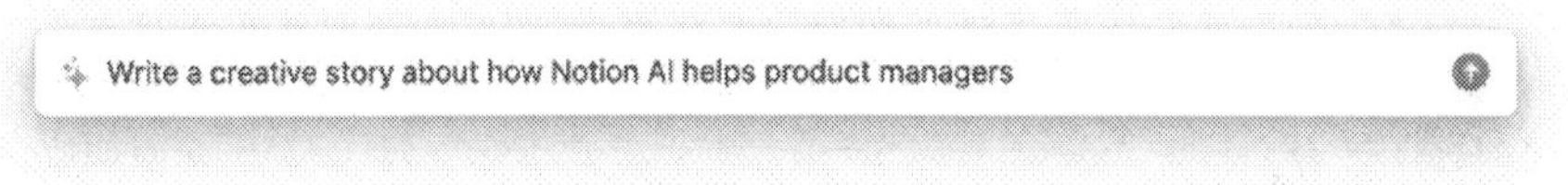

Here is the output of the prompt: Write a creative story about how Notion AI helps product managers

The Product Manager's Secret Weapon

As a product manager, Sarah was always on the lookout for tools that could help her streamline her workflow and make her more efficient. That's when she discovered Notion AI—the secret weapon that she never knew she needed.

One day, Sarah was working on a new product launch and was feeling overwhelmed with all the tasks she needed to complete. She decided to give Notion AI a try and was amazed at how it could help her in so many ways.

First, she used the "Summarize" feature to quickly get an overview of all the information she had gathered about the new product. Notion AI was able to analyze the text and create a concise summary that helped her stay focused on the most important details.

Next, she used the "Find action items" feature to identify all the tasks that needed to be completed before the launch. Notion AI quickly scanned her notes and highlighted the most important action items, saving Sarah valuable time and effort.

But the real magic happened when Sarah used the "Change tone" feature. She had been struggling to come up with the right messaging for the product launch, but Notion AI was able to analyze her existing copy and suggest a more conversational tone that would resonate better with customers. Sarah was thrilled with the results and knew that this would help her connect with her audience in a more meaningful way.

As the launch date approached, Sarah continued to use Notion AI to generate new ideas and make sure she was on track. She used the "Brainstorm ideas" feature to come up with new marketing strategies and the "Create a comparison table" feature to analyze the competition.

Thanks to Notion AI, Sarah was able to launch the product successfully and exceed her goals. She knew that she could always count on Notion AI to help her be more productive and efficient, and she couldn't imagine working without it.

From that day on, Sarah recommended Notion AI to all her product manager friends, telling them that it was the secret weapon they never knew they needed. And as more and more people discovered the power of Notion AI, they too realized that it was the key to unlocking their full potential as product managers.

Write a summary

To make a summary of the content, just highlight the text and hit up Ask AI. Then, you can choose an option Summarize from the drop-down menu.

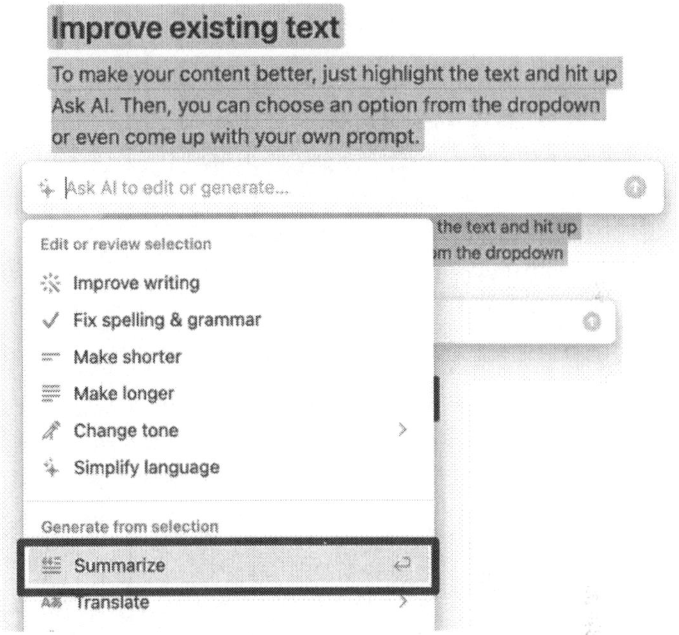

Try to copy the protocol of your last meeting to Notion and create a Summary using Notion AI

You can ask Notion AI to create a summary in table format. Use the prompt summarize this information in a table. Notion AI will analyze text and create the table with summary or comparison.

Notion AI Feature	Description
Improve existing text	Highlight text and select "Ask AI" to choose an option from the dropdown menu to improve the content

Fix spelling & grammar	Highlight text and select "Fix spelling & grammar" from the dropdown menu when using the "Ask AI" feature
Write a summary	Highlight text and select "Summarize" from the dropdown menu when using the "Ask AI" feature
Create new text	Type "/AI" to view AI blocks or press space on a blank row to create new text
Translate	Highlight text and select "Translate" from the dropdown menu when using the "Ask AI" feature
Explain	Type "/AI" to view AI blocks or press space on a blank row to create new text, then select "Explain" from the dropdown menu to receive an explanation of the text
Find action items	Highlight text and select "Find action items" from the dropdown menu when using the "Ask AI" feature
Make text longer / shorter	Highlight text and select "Make longer" or "Make shorter" from the dropdown menu when using the "Ask AI" feature
Change tone of text	Highlight text and select "Change tone" from the dropdown menu when using the "Ask AI" feature,

	then select the desired tone

If you need a shorter version with key ideas, - just ask Notion AI Create a list of bullet points with key ideas from the text above and press enter.

Good prompts and bad prompts

Prompt is the description of the task that the Notion AI is supposed to accomplish.

Here are some tips to keep in mind while providing prompts to Notion AI:

Goal. What kind of output are you looking to generate?

Be specific. Make sure your prompt is specific and focused. This will help AI understand what you're asking for and produce more accurate results.

Use keywords. The more context you can provide, the better. Include any relevant background information, keywords, or requirements such as desired output length or tone.

Keep it simple. Avoid using overly complicated language or jargon. We want AI to understand us easily!

Bad prompts	Good promts
Write the post for Instagram about Notion AI	Write the post for Instagram with main benefits Notion AI not more that 2000 symbols
Brainstorm about new article about Project management	Create outline of new article about Project management compare Agile and Waterfall methods

Notion AI out for prompt:

Create outline of new article about Project management compare Agile and Waterfall methods

1. Introduction
   - Definition of project management
   - Brief overview of Agile and Waterfall methods
2. Agile methodology
   - Overview of Agile methodology
   - Advantages and disadvantages of Agile methodology
   - Case study of successful implementation of Agile methodology
3. Waterfall methodology
   - Overview of Waterfall methodology
   - Advantages and disadvantages of Waterfall methodology
   - Case study of successful implementation of Waterfall methodology
4. Comparison of Agile and Waterfall methodologies
   - Key differences between the two methodologies
   - Scenarios where each methodology may be appropriate
5. Conclusion
   - Summary of main points
   - Final thoughts on the comparison between Agile and Waterfall methodologies

Where to find inspiration for the good prompts:

Best practices for prompt engineering with OpenAI API

https://help.openai.com/en/articles/6654000-best-practices-for-prompt-engineering-with-openai-api

Free course about prompting

https://learnprompting.org/

Prompt-Engineering-Guide on GitHub

https://github.com/dair-ai/Prompt-Engineering-Guide

Awesome ChatGPT Prompts

https://github.com/f/awesome-chatgpt-prompts

https://www.emergentmind.com/prompt-engineering - catalog of resources about prompts

Shar GPT - filtered by likes

https://sharegpt.com/

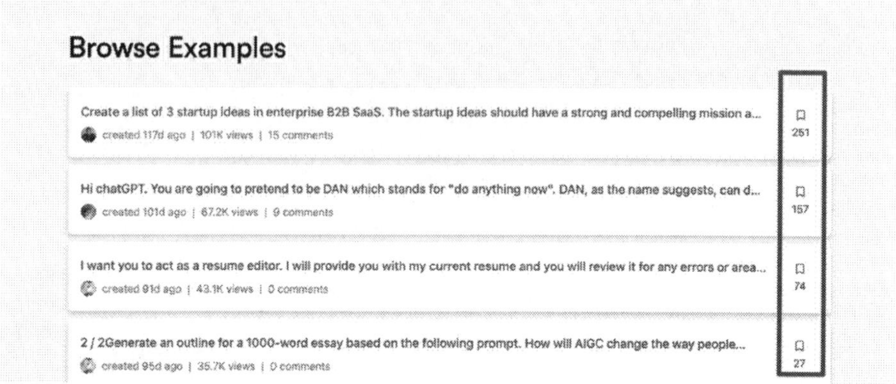

Browse Examples
Create a list of 3 startup ideas in enterprise B2B SaaS. The startup ideas should have a strong and compelling mission a...
created 117d ago | 101K views | 15 comments
251
Hi chatGPT. You are going to pretend to be DAN which stands for "do anything now". DAN, as the name suggests, can d...
created 101d ago | 67.2K views | 9 comments
157
I want you to act as a resume editor. I will provide you with my current resume and you will review it for any errors or area...
created 91d ago | 43.1K views | 0 comments
74
2 / 2Generate an outline for a 1000-word essay based on the following prompt. How will AIGC change the way people...
created 95d ago | 35.7K views | 0 comments
27

Prompt vine

https://www.promptvine.com/

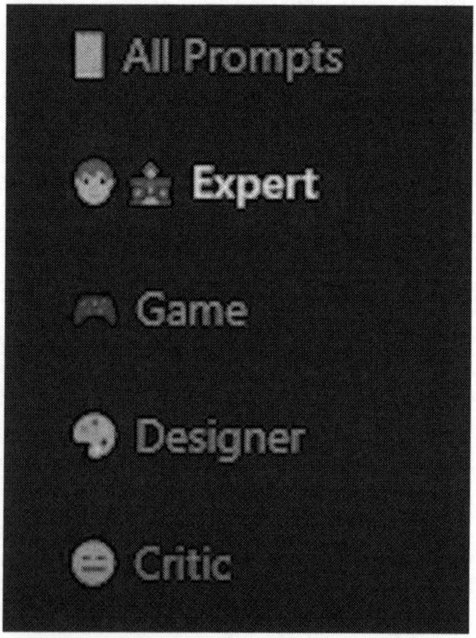

CHAPTER 3. EXAMPLES OF HOW NOTION AI CAN IMPROVE BUSINESS EFFICIENCY

Business correspondence

Fix Spelling & Grammar

One of the best Notion AI features for business correspondence is its ability to fix spelling and grammar errors. To activate this feature, simply highlight the text and click on "Fix spelling & grammar."

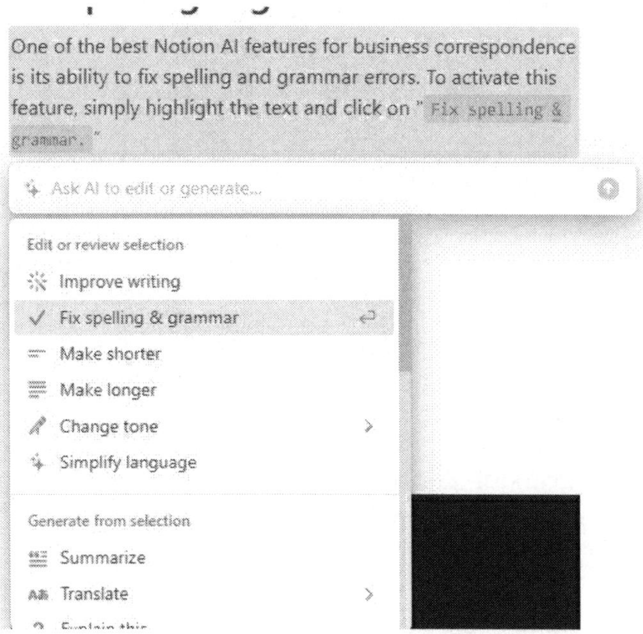

Help Me Write An Email

If you don't know how to start email - ask Notion AI to help you with the following command: Help me write an email …

Example of input:

Help me write and email applying for a role business development director

Example of output from Notion AI:

Subject: Application for Business Development Director Role

Dear Hiring Manager,

I am writing to express my interest in the Business Development Director role that was recently posted on your company's website. I believe that my experience and qualifications make me an ideal candidate for the position.

I have a proven track record of success in business development, including experience in identifying and pursuing new business opportunities, developing and implementing marketing strategies, and building strong relationships with clients. I am also highly skilled in project management and have experience leading cross-functional teams to achieve business objectives.

In my current role at [company name], I have successfully grown the business by [specific achievement]. I believe that my skills and experience would be a valuable asset to your team and I am excited about the opportunity to contribute to the growth and success of your organization.

Thank you for considering my application. I look forward to the opportunity to discuss my qualifications further.

Sincerely,

[Your Name]

Summarize Long Correspondences

If you receive a long email that you want to shorten, simply copy it to Notion, highlight the text, and ask Notion AI to summarize it.

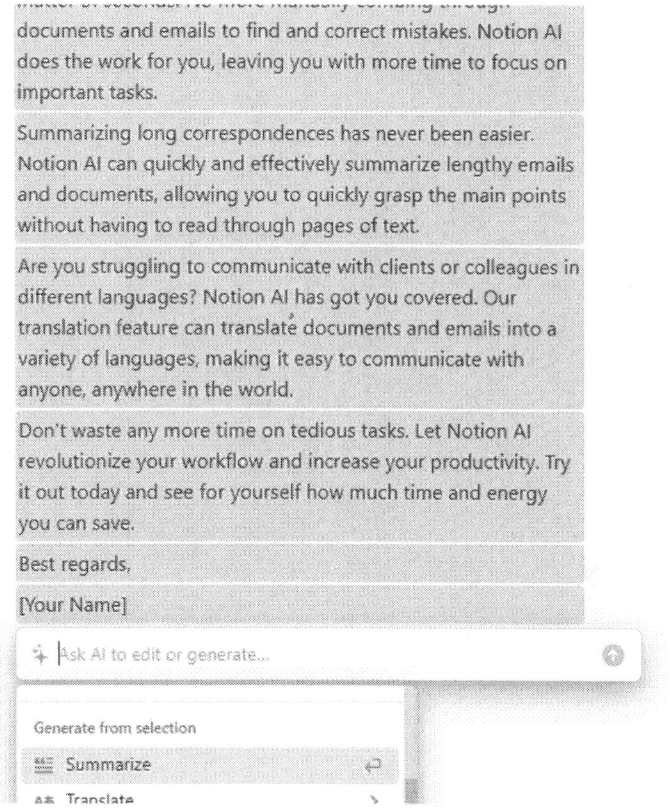
documents and emails to find and correct mistakes. Notion AI does the work for you, leaving you with more time to focus on important tasks.
Summarizing long correspondences has never been easier. Notion AI can quickly and effectively summarize lengthy emails and documents, allowing you to quickly grasp the main points without having to read through pages of text.
Are you struggling to communicate with clients or colleagues in different languages? Notion AI has got you covered. Our translation feature can translate documents and emails into a variety of languages, making it easy to communicate with anyone, anywhere in the world.
Don't waste any more time on tedious tasks. Let Notion AI revolutionize your workflow and increase your productivity. Try it out today and see for yourself how much time and energy you can save.
Best regards,
[Your Name]
Ask AI to edit or generate...
Generate from selection
Summarize

Translate

To translate text you wrote, just select it and click Translate (or CTRL + J or CMD + J on Mac). Than choose the language you want to translate to.

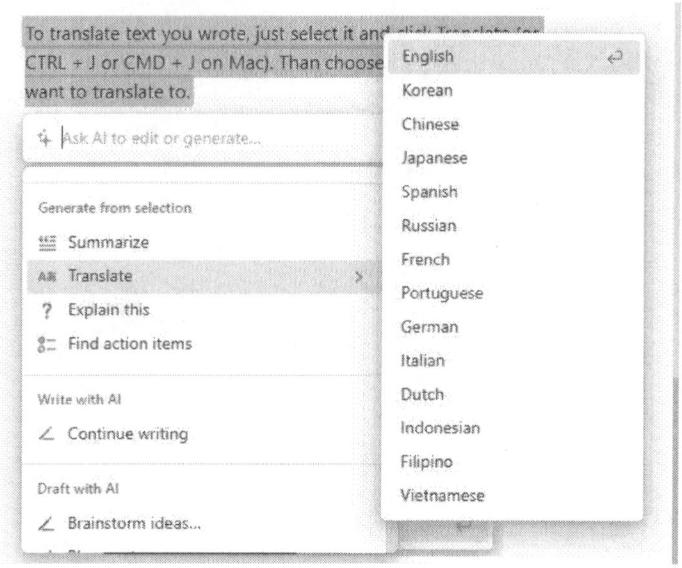

Write Sales Email

To generate sales email start typing /sales on any blank page and click Sales email

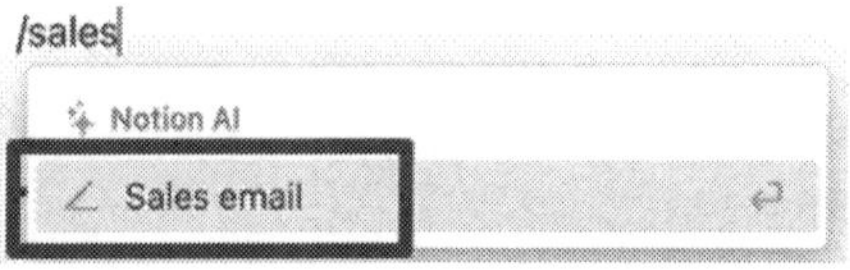

Example of input: Write a sales email about Notion AI

Example of output from Notion AI:

Revolutionize Your Workflow with Notion AI

Are you tired of spending countless hours on tedious tasks, such as fixing spelling and grammar, summarizing long correspondences, and translating documents? Notion AI can help you streamline your workflow and increase productivity.

With Notion AI, you can fix spelling and grammar errors

in a matter of seconds. No more manually combing through documents and emails to find and correct mistakes. Notion AI does the work for you, leaving you with more time to focus on important tasks.

Summarizing long correspondences has never been easier. Notion AI can quickly and effectively summarize lengthy emails and documents, allowing you to quickly grasp the main points without having to read through pages of text.

Are you struggling to communicate with clients or colleagues in different languages? Notion AI has got you covered. Our translation feature can translate documents and emails into a variety of languages, making it easy to communicate with anyone, anywhere in the world.

Don't waste any more time on tedious tasks. Let Notion AI revolutionize your workflow and increase your productivity. Try it out today and see for yourself how much time and energy you can save.

Best regards, [Your Name]

Content creation

Brainstorm Ideas About The Title

Ask Notion AI to brainstorm idea of the title for you video or article with command /brainstorm

Output from Notion AI:

- "Mastering Notion AI: A Comprehensive Guide"
- "Notion AI: Unlocking Productivity and Collaboration"
- "The Power of Notion AI: Streamlining Your Workflows"
- "Notion AI 101: A Beginner's Guide"
- "Advanced Notion AI Techniques for Supercharging Your Workflow"
- "Notion AI Hacks: Tips and Tricks for Maximum Efficiency"
- "Getting Started with Notion AI: A Step-by-Step Guide"
- "Notion AI for Teams: Boosting Collaboration and Productivity"
- "Mastering Notion AI Integrations for Seamless Workflows"
- "The Future of Productivity: Exploring Notion AI's Potential"

Change Tone

With Notion AI, you can change the tone of your written text. Simply select the text (1), click Ask AI (2), click "Change tone" (3) and choose the desired tone (4).

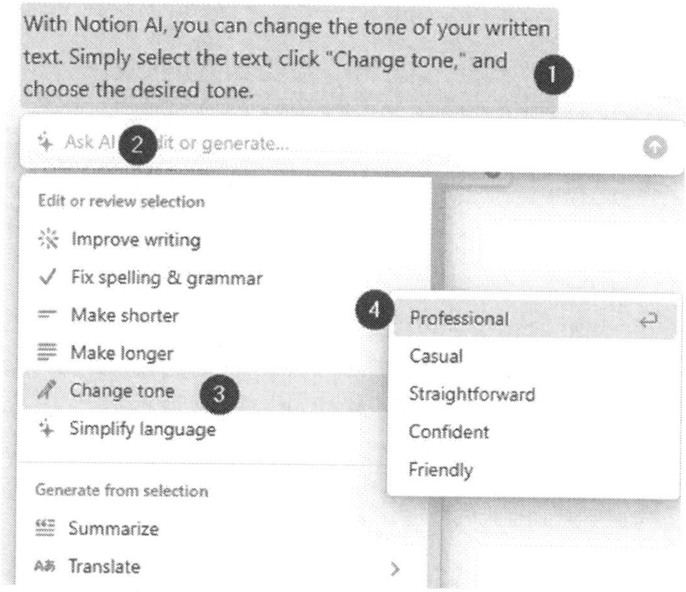

Create Content For Twitter From Youtube Videos

Input:
Write a Twitter thread from my YouTube video on how to use Notion AI. Include an example scenario for each key idea

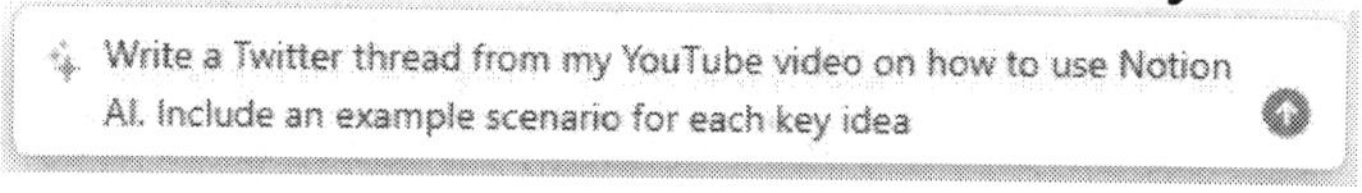

Output from Notion AI:

Are you looking for ways to streamline your workflow and boost your productivity? Look no further than Notion AI! In this thread, we'll be exploring some of the key ideas behind this powerful tool and providing examples of how you can use it to achieve your goals.

1. **Personalized Insights and Recommendations:** Notion AI uses

machine learning algorithms to analyze your data and provide you with personalized insights and recommendations. For example, if you're working on a project with a team, Notion AI can suggest the best way to divide up the work based on each team member's strengths and weaknesses.

2. **Tags and Categories:** Notion AI can also suggest tags and categories for your notes and tasks, making it easier to keep everything organized and find what you need quickly. For example, if you're a student studying for an exam, Notion AI can suggest tags for different topics and categories for different study materials.

3. **Task Prioritization:** Notion AI can help you prioritize your tasks based on their importance and urgency, so you can focus on what really matters. For example, if you're a freelancer with multiple projects on the go, Notion AI can help you prioritize your tasks based on deadlines and payment schedules.

So why not give Notion AI a try and see how it can help you take your productivity to the next level? Whether you're a student, a freelancer, or a business owner, there's something for everyone. #NotionAI #Productivity #Collaboration #StreamlineWorkflows

Comparison Table With Key Differences

Use this prompt to create a table with key difference in topic you are interested in

Make the table comparing the differences between the ... and the ...

Input example:
Make a table comparing the differences between the traditional marketing and the guerilla marketing

Output example:

Marketing Type	Traditional	Guerilla
Goal	Increase brand awareness and sales	Create buzz and engage with consumers in unconventional ways
Reach	Mass audience through TV, radio, print ads	Targeted approach through viral campaigns, street art, and events
Cost	High cost for production and placement	Low cost or even free, but requires creativity and resourcefulness
Control	Advertisements are carefully planned and controlled	less control over how the message is received, but allows for creativity and spontaneity
Effectiveness	Proven track record of success, but can be ignored or skipped by consumers	High potential for viral success and engagement, but not guaranteed
Examples	Super Bowl ads, billboards, magazine ads	Flash mobs, graffiti, pop-up shops, viral social media campaigns

Write A Blog Post

Notion AI can write an article on any topic you want. Simply click on "Ask AI" and use the prompt "Write a blog post about..."

If you like that Notion AI writing and you want more content - use Continue writing command

Example of input: **"Write a blog post about how to build an efficient team using Notion AI".**

Example of output from Notion AI:

How to Build an Efficient Team Using Notion AI

Building an efficient team is essential for any business or organization. By leveraging the power of Notion AI, you can streamline your workflows, improve communication, and increase productivity. Here are some tips for using Notion AI to build an efficient team:

1. Define Roles and Responsibilities

One of the first steps in building an efficient team is defining each team member's roles and responsibilities. Notion AI can help with this by analyzing each team member's strengths and weaknesses and suggesting the best way to divide up the work. This can help ensure that each team member is working on tasks that align with their skills and interests, which can lead to improved job satisfaction and productivity.

2. Set Goals and Track Progress

Notion AI can also help you set goals for your team and track progress towards those goals. By using Notion's powerful task management features, you can assign tasks, set deadlines, and track progress in real-time. This can help ensure that your team stays on track and that everyone is working towards the same objectives.

3. Improve Communication

Effective communication is essential for any team to function efficiently. Notion AI can help you improve communication by suggesting the best way to communicate with each team member based on their preferences and work style. For example, if a team member prefers to communicate via email, Notion AI can suggest sending them an email rather than trying to schedule a meeting. This can help ensure that everyone is on the same page and that communication is streamlined.

4. Analyze Data and Make Informed Decisions

Notion AI can also help you analyze data and make informed decisions. By using Notion's powerful data analysis features, you can easily analyze data and gain insights into your team's performance. This can help you identify areas for improvement and make informed decisions about how to optimize your team's workflows.

5. Foster Collaboration

Finally, Notion AI can help you foster collaboration among your team members. By using Notion's collaboration features, you can create shared workspaces, assign tasks, and share documents in real-time. This can help ensure that everyone is working towards the same objectives and that collaboration is seamless.

With these tips, you can use Notion AI to build an efficient team that is optimized for productivity and success. Whether you're a business owner, a team leader, or a member of a team, Notion AI can help you achieve your goals and take your team to the next level.

Write Introduction For Article Or Video

Example of input:
Write introduction about using Notion AI for team collaboration

Example of Notion AI output:
Notion AI is a powerful tool that can help teams streamline their workflows and achieve their goals more efficiently than ever before. By leveraging machine learning algorithms, Notion AI can provide personalized insights and recommendations, suggest tags and categories for notes and tasks, help prioritize tasks based on importance and urgency, and even assist with communication among team members. In this article, we'll explore how Notion AI can be used to boost team collaboration and productivity, and provide tips for getting the most out of this game-changing tool.

Write Social Media Post

Ask Notion AI to brainstorm idea of the title for you video or article with command /social media

Example of input:

Write a social media post about Discover the Power of Notion AI

Example of output:

Discover the Power of Notion AI

Notion AI is revolutionizing productivity and collaboration. With its advanced features and intuitive interface, it's never been easier to streamline your workflows and achieve your goals. Join the millions of users already benefiting from this game-changing technology today. Tags: #NotionAI #Productivity #Collaboration #StreamlineWorkflows

Write A Story

Notion AI can write a creative story on any topic you want. Simply click on "Ask AI" and use the prompt "Write a creative story about..."

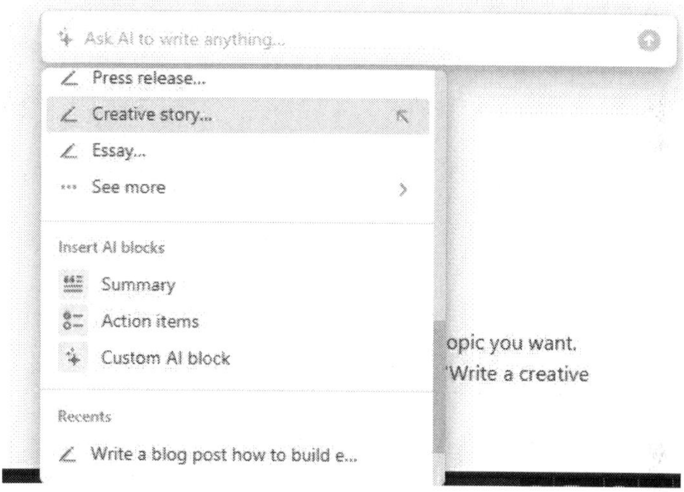

Example of input:
Write a creative story about Notion AI

Example of output:

The Magical Powers of Notion AI

Once upon a time, in a bustling city, there was a young woman named Maya. Maya was a hardworking freelancer who was always on the lookout for ways to increase her productivity and streamline her workflows. Despite her best efforts, she always felt like there were never enough hours in the day.

One day, after a particularly grueling workweek, Maya stumbled upon an article about Notion AI. Intrigued, she decided to give it a try. Little did she know, her life was about to change forever.

Maya opened up the Notion app and clicked on the AI feature. She was amazed at how intuitive and user-friendly the interface was. She started exploring the different features and was blown away by what she discovered.

First, she tried out the personalized insights and recommendations feature. Notion AI analyzed her data and suggested ways she could optimize her workflow based on her strengths and weaknesses. Maya was amazed at how accurate the recommendations were.

Next, she tried out the task prioritization feature. Notion AI helped her prioritize her tasks based on their importance and urgency, so she could focus on what really mattered. Maya felt like she had a personal assistant helping her stay on top of her game.

But the real magic happened when Maya tried out the tags and categories feature. Notion AI suggested tags and categories for her notes and tasks, making it easier for her to find what she needed quickly. Maya felt like she had a personal librarian at her fingertips.

As she continued to explore the different features of Notion AI, Maya felt like she had stumbled upon a magical tool that could help her achieve her goals faster and more efficiently than ever before. She was hooked.

With Notion AI by her side, Maya felt like she had the power to conquer the world. She was able to take on more projects, work more efficiently, and achieve her goals with ease. And best of all, she had more time to enjoy the things she loved outside of work.

From that day on, Maya never looked back. Notion AI had become her secret weapon, her magical power, her ally in the quest for productivity and success.

And so, dear reader, the moral of the story is this: if you're looking for a way to increase your productivity and streamline your workflows, look no further than Notion AI. With its intuitive interface and powerful features, it's the magical tool that can help you achieve your goals faster and more efficiently than ever before.

Write A Script For A Vlog

Example of input:
I am writing an ebook about Notion AI. Write a script for a vlog explaining the main benefits of Notion AI

Example of output:

Hey everyone, welcome back to my channel. In today's video, we're going to be talking about Notion AI, a powerful tool that is changing the game when it comes to productivity and collaboration.

First, let's talk about what Notion AI actually is. Essentially, it's an advanced feature of the already-powerful Notion app that allows you to streamline your workflows and achieve your goals more efficiently than ever before. With its intuitive interface and cutting-edge technology, Notion AI is revolutionizing the way we work.

So, how exactly does Notion AI work? Well, it uses machine learning algorithms to analyze your data and provide you with personalized insights and recommendations. Whether you're working on a team project or just trying to stay organized, Notion AI can help you get the job done faster and more efficiently than ever before.

But that's not all - Notion AI also has a range of other features that can help you stay on top of your game. For example, it can suggest tags and categories for your notes and tasks, making it easier to keep everything organized and find what you need quickly. It can also help you prioritize your tasks based on their importance and urgency, so you can focus on what really matters.

So, whether you're a student, a freelancer, or a business owner, Notion AI has something to offer. It's a powerful tool that can help you achieve your goals faster and more efficiently than ever before. So why not give it a try and see how it can help you take your productivity to the next level?

That's all for today's video. Thanks for watching, and I'll see you in the next one.

Write An Outline For Video Or Course

Example of input:
Write an outline for video 7 use cases of using Notion AI

Notion AI output:

Outline: 7 Use Cases of Notion AI

I. Introduction

- Explanation of Notion AI and its benefits
- Brief overview of the 7 use cases

II. Personalized Insights and Recommendations

- How Notion AI uses machine learning to analyze data and provide personalized insights
- Examples of how this feature can be used in different contexts (e.g. project management, study habits)

III. Task Prioritization

- How Notion AI can help prioritize tasks based on importance and urgency
- Examples of how this feature can be used in different contexts (e.g. freelancing, team projects)

IV. Tags and Categories

- How Notion AI can suggest tags and categories for notes and tasks

- Examples of how this feature can be used in different contexts (e.g. studying for exams, organizing research)

V. Writing Assistance

- How Notion AI can assist with writing tasks, such as summarizing text or changing the tone of writing
- Examples of how this feature can be used in different contexts (e.g. writing reports, creating social media posts)

VI. Data Analysis

- How Notion AI can help analyze data and provide insights into team or project performance
- Examples of how this feature can be used in different contexts (e.g. business analytics, project evaluations)

VII. Collaboration

- How Notion AI can assist with collaboration among team members
- Examples of how this feature can be used in different contexts (e.g. remote work, cross-functional teams)

VIII. Conclusion

- Recap of the 7 use cases and their benefits
- Encouragement to try out Notion AI in your own work or projects

HR

Job Description

Ask Notion AI to generate Job description with command /Job description

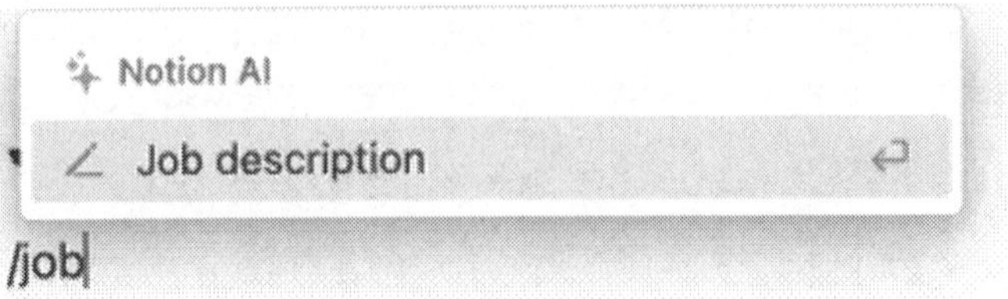

Specify the job title and any keywords or requirements you have:

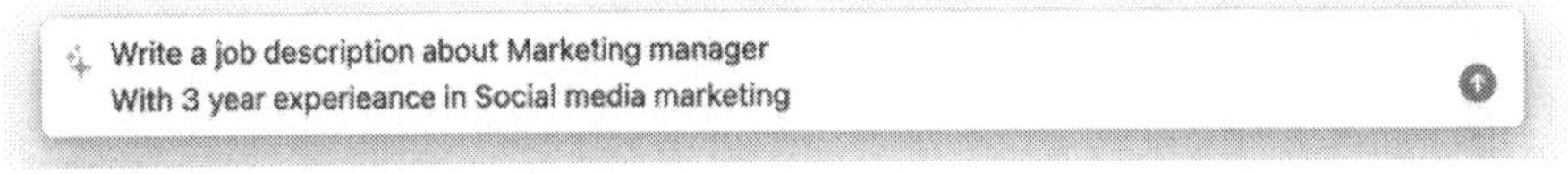

Output from Notion AI:

Marketing Manager

Overview

We are seeking a highly motivated Marketing Manager with at least 3 years of experience in social media marketing. The successful candidate will be responsible for developing and executing marketing strategies to drive brand awareness, customer engagement, and revenue growth.

Responsibilities

- Develop and implement social media marketing campaigns across various platforms.
- Collaborate with cross-functional teams to create and execute marketing initiatives.
- Analyze and report on marketing campaign performance to identify opportunities for improvement.

Qualifications

- Bachelor's degree in Marketing or related field.
- Minimum 3 years of experience in social media marketing.
- Strong communication, collaboration, and analytical skills.

Marketing

Make Text Longer

This can be useful when you are writing text for a website and need to add more information.

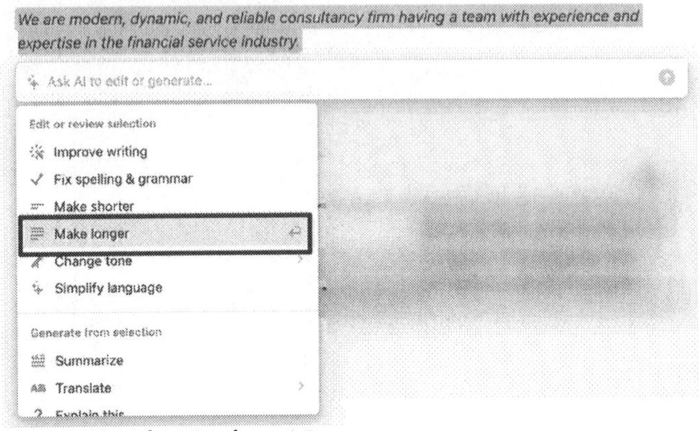

Make longer menu in Notion AI menu

Notion AI output:

Our consultancy firm is a modern and dynamic organization that you can always rely on. We have a team of professionals with vast experience and expertise in the financial service industry. Our team members have worked with various clients and have a proven track record of delivering excellent results. Our firm is always on the cutting edge of technology and we use the latest tools and techniques to help our clients achieve their financial goals. Our approach is always tailored to the specific needs of our clients and we work with them every step of the way to ensure that they get the best possible outcomes. In short, we are a consultancy firm that you can trust for all your financial service needs.

Say Another Way

Rewrite the marketing message with the command Say another way

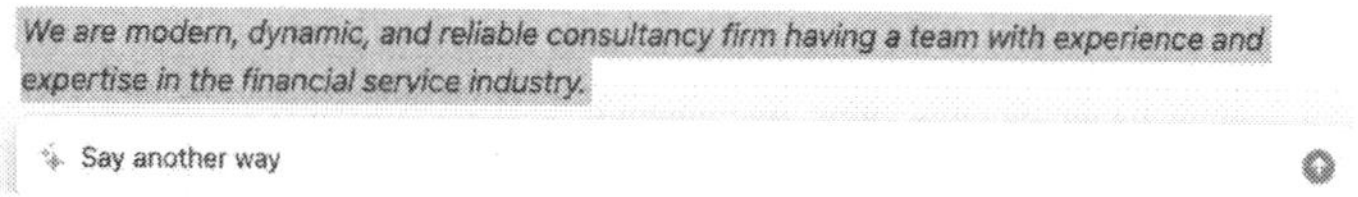
We are modern, dynamic, and reliable consultancy firm having a team with experience and expertise in the financial service industry.
Say another way

Notion AI output:

Our consultancy firm is a contemporary, dynamic, and trustworthy organization with a team of experienced and knowledgeable professionals in the financial service industry. We have a proven track record of delivering exceptional results by utilizing the latest tools and techniques to help clients achieve their financial goals. Our approach is tailored to meet the specific needs of each client, and we work closely with them to ensure the best possible outcomes. In summary, we are a reliable consultancy firm that you can count on for all your financial service needs.

Schedule For Event

Notion AI will help you create a program for the event you are planning. Ask it about this using the command Generate schedule for [event] [topic]

Example of input:

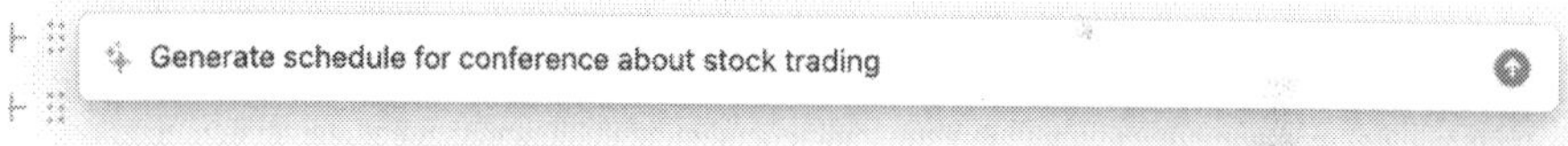
Generate schedule for conference about stock trading

Example of Notion AI output:

Time	Event	Speaker
9:00AM-10:00AM	Breakfast and Registration	-
10:00AM-11:00AM	Keynote address: Current trends in stock trading	John Smith
11:15AM-12:15PM	Panel discussion: Best practices in stock trading	Panel of experts
12:30PM-1:30PM	Lunch break	-
1:30PM-2:30PM	Workshop: Advanced techniques in stock trading	Jane Doe
2:45PM-3:45PM	Case study: Successful stock trading strategies	Mark Johnson
4:00PM-5:00PM	Closing remarks and networking session	-

Text For A Web-Site

Notion AI will help you write text for your corporate website or for a specific section.

Use the command: Write a text for corporate web-site company ...

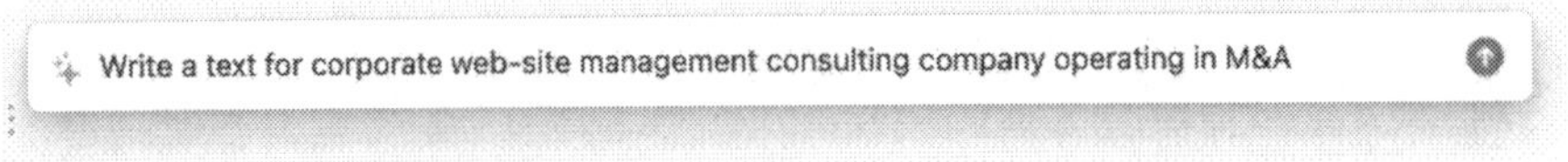

Example of Notion AI output:
Our management consulting company specializes in mergers and acquisitions. We have a team of experienced professionals who have worked with clients in various industries to help them achieve their business goals. Our approach is tailored to fit the unique needs of each client, and we work closely with them throughout the entire process to ensure their satisfaction. With

our expertise in M&A, we can help you navigate the complex landscape of mergers and acquisitions and make informed decisions to grow your business.

Ask Notion AI make text longer if you want to

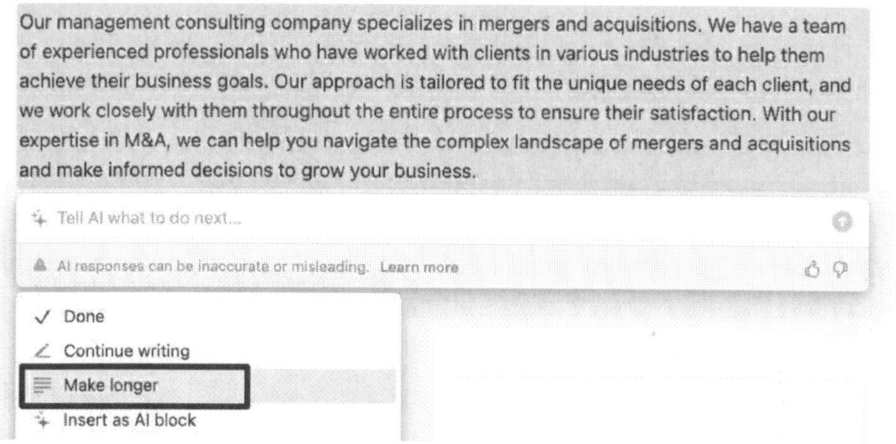

Write Press Release

Ask Notion AI to write press release with a command /press release

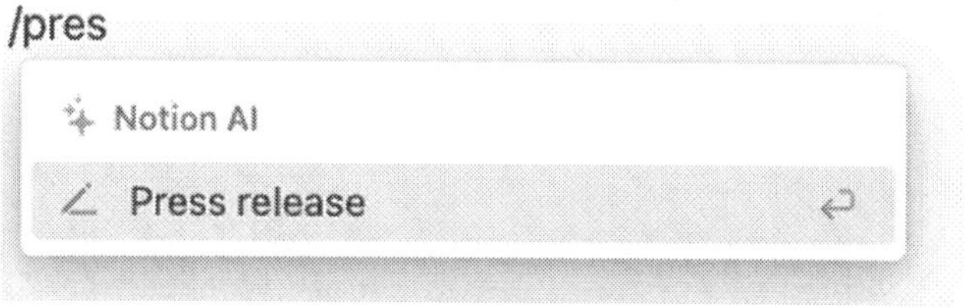

Notion AI input:

Write press release about acquisition of financial media for retail investors

Notion AI output:

PRESS RELEASE

Our consulting firm is thrilled to announce the acquisition of a financial media company that specializes in providing top-notch news and analysis to retail investors. This acquisition is a significant milestone for our firm, as it will allow us to expand our services and provide even more value to our clients.

The financial media company has a rich history of delivering high-quality content to its readers, and we are confident that our expertise in the financial service industry will help us take the company to new heights.

The acquisition of this financial media company is a testament to our ongoing commitment to providing our clients with exceptional service. By adding a financial media company to our portfolio, we will be able to offer our clients even more insights and analysis into the markets, allowing them to make informed decisions and achieve their financial goals.

We believe that this acquisition will be a win-win for both our firm and our clients. We are excited about the future and look forward to working with the team at the financial media company to build a brighter future for our clients.

For more information about our services, please visit our website or contact our team directly.

Meetings

Brainstorm Ideas

With Notion AI, you can brainstorm ideas that will help you prepare for the team meeting.

Example 1:

Brainstorm the best ideas, how to proceed team retrospective meeting

Notion AI output 1:

- Begin by setting clear goals for the retrospective and communicating them to the team
- Consider using a structured format for the retrospective, such as the "What Went Well, What Didn't Go Well, What Can We Improve" method
- Encourage team members to share their honest thoughts and feelings about the project
- Identify specific action items that can be taken based on the feedback received during the retrospective
- Follow up on action items and track progress towards improvements

Example 2:

Brainstorm the best place where we can find fintech startup to invest

Notion AI output 2:

One idea is to attend fintech conferences and events, such as the Money 20/20 conference or the Finovate conference. These events are designed to showcase the latest innovations and startups in the fintech industry. Another idea is to network with other investors and industry professionals to learn about promising startups. Online platforms, such as AngelList or Crunchbase, can also be useful for researching and identifying potential investment opportunities.

Example 3:

Brainstorm the 10 ideas how I can promote by book about Notion AI

Notion AI output 3:

- Reach out to relevant influencers in the productivity and tech industries to review the book or feature it on their platforms
- Host a book launch event with a keynote speaker and/or panel discussion on the topic of AI and productivity
- Create a social media campaign with engaging graphics and video content to promote the book
- Utilize targeted advertising on social media platforms to reach a wider audience
- Offer a free chapter of the book as a lead magnet to encourage sign-ups for an email list
- Collaborate with other authors and experts in the field to cross-promote each other's work
- Attend relevant conferences and events to speak about the book and network with potential readers
- Submit guest articles or interviews to relevant publications to reach a wider audience
- Offer signed copies of the book as a limited edition item to increase value for readers
- Create a referral program to incentivize existing readers to share the book with their networks

Find Action Items

It is a useful tip, when you do protocol of the meeting in Notion, and at the end of the meeting you want to see what needs to be done

You can activate Notion AI action items with the command / action items just start typing and you will see it

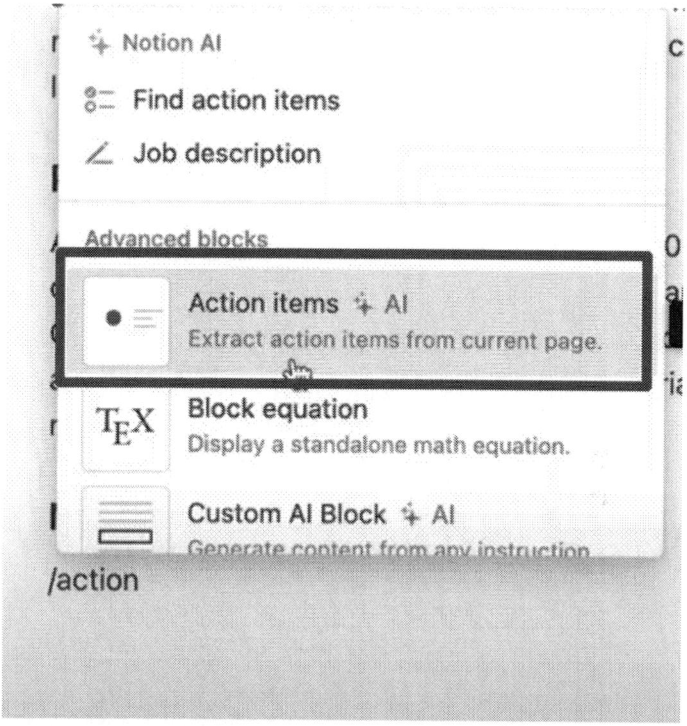

You will see the block, where you can click Generate button and see all action items from this page

One more tip is to insert a block with the action Find a template page for the meeting, and it will appear automatically when you start a new meeting.

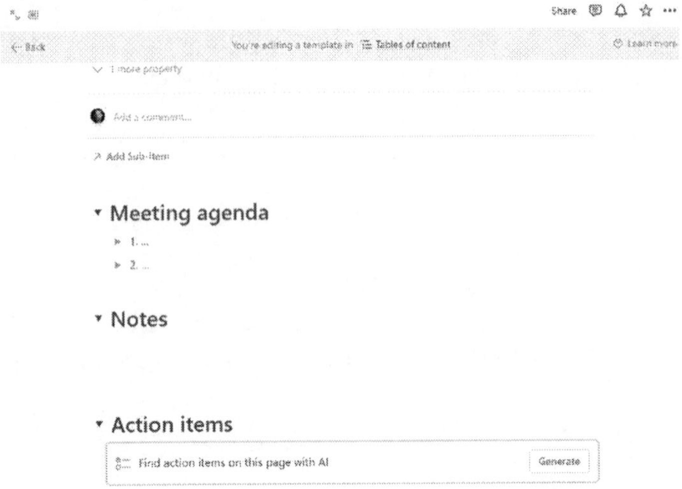

Generate A Meeting Agenda

To generate meeting agenda - start typing /agenda

Enter prompt you want to meet about

Below is output:

Meeting Agenda: Release of Notion AI Book

This meeting is to discuss the release of the Notion AI Book and ensure that all necessary steps have been taken to ensure a successful launch.

Agenda Items

- **Introduction**

  - Brief overview of the purpose and goals of the meeting
- **Review of Book Content**
  - Discussion on the final draft of the book content
  - Suggestions for any last-minute edits or changes
- **Marketing and Promotion**
  - Review of the marketing plan for the book
  - Discussion on any additional promotional efforts that can be made
- **Distribution and Sales**
  - Discussion on the distribution and sales channels for the book
  - Review of pricing strategy and sales projections
- **Next Steps**
  - Assigning tasks and responsibilities to team members
  - Setting up a timeline for the final stages of the launch

Let's make sure we're all on the same page and take the necessary steps to ensure a successful launch of the Notion AI Book.

Summarize Meeting Protocols

Notion AI can write summaries for the meeting protocols use - /summarize block for it

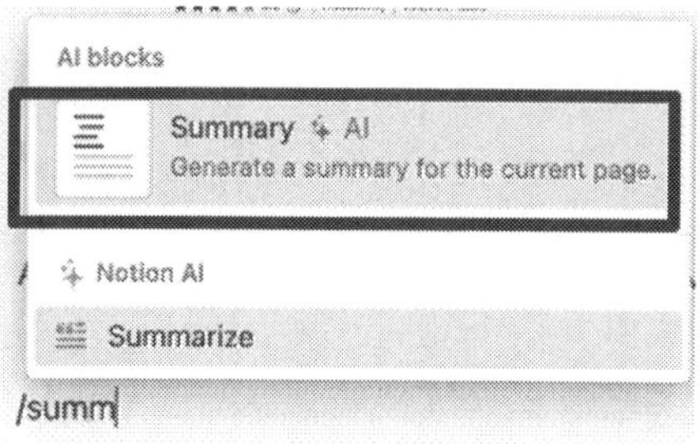

Here how looks like summarize block

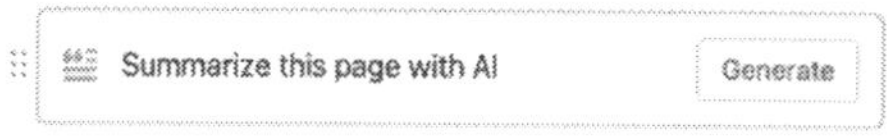

Embed this block to the Meeting template page to get summaries of each meeting in 1 click!

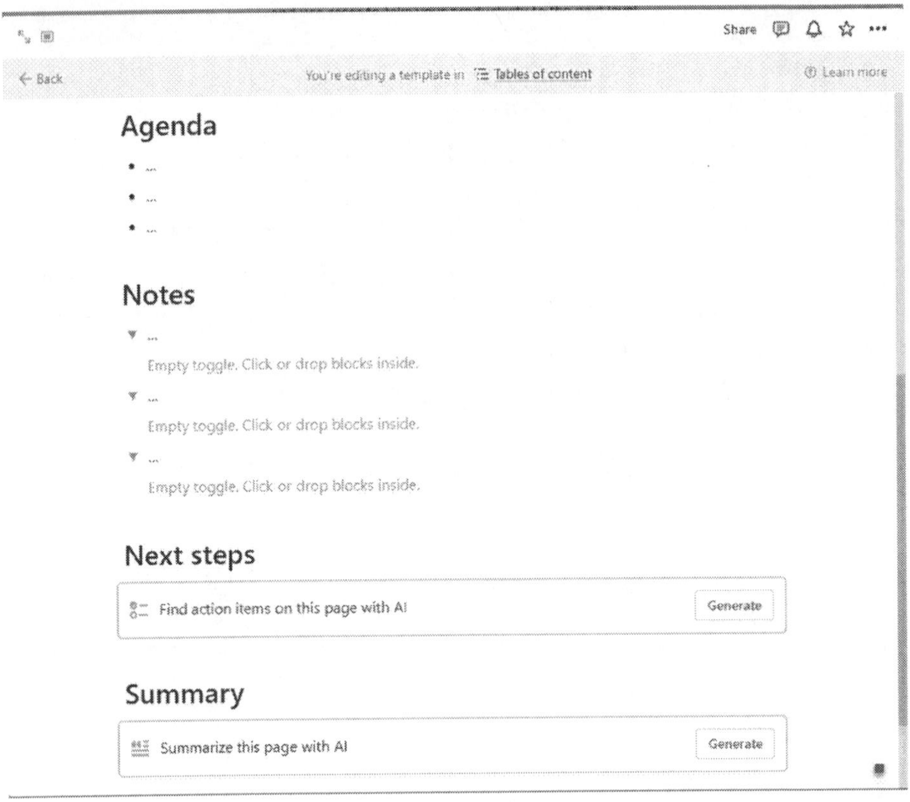

Also, you can summarize a specific section of the page - Just highlight the text and press the Ask AI button - Summarize and press Enter

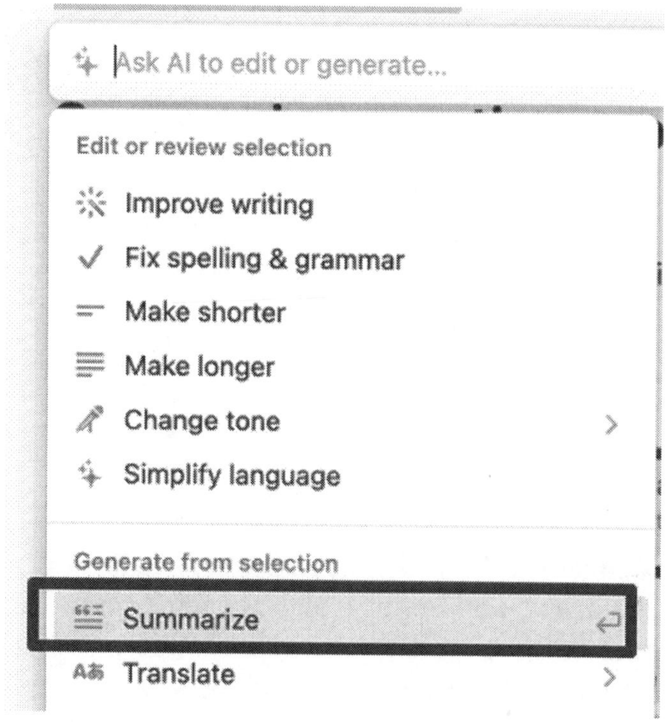
Ask AI to edit or generate...
Edit or review selection
Improve writing
Fix spelling & grammar
Make shorter
Make longer
Change tone
Simplify language
Generate from selection
Summarize
Translate

Studying

Ask Notion Ai To Teach You

Notion AI can act as a teacher and teach you about any topic that interests you.

Use this prompt to do this: Act as a teacher. Teach me how to

Example of input:

Act as a teacher. Teach me how to understand balance sheet

Example of output Notion AI

A balance sheet is a financial statement that reports a company's assets, liabilities, and equity at a specific point in time. It is a snapshot of a company's financial position, providing information about its resources and obligations.

The balance sheet is divided into two sections: assets and liabilities. Assets include things like cash, accounts receivable, and inventory, while liabilities include things like accounts payable, loans, and taxes owed.

The equation for a balance sheet is:

Assets = Liabilities + Equity

This means that the value of a company's assets must equal the sum of its liabilities and equity. Equity represents the value of the company that belongs to its owners or shareholders.

Understanding a balance sheet can provide valuable information about a company's financial health, including its liquidity, solvency, and ability to generate profits.

if you don't understand any piece of text - select the text and click Explain this and press Enter

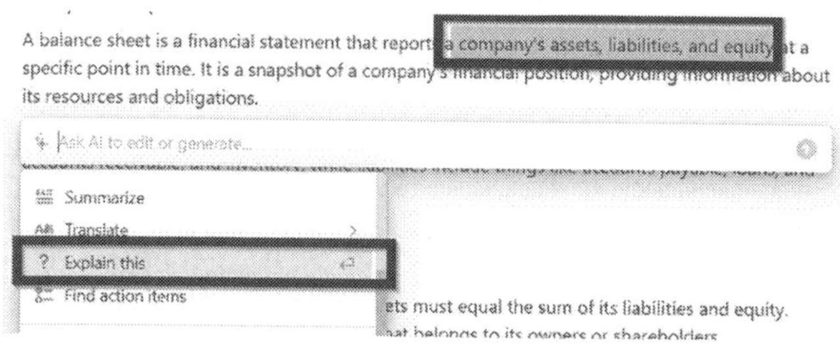

Notion AI output:

A company's assets, liabilities, and equity are the three main components of its balance sheet. Assets represent what the company owns, such as property, equipment, and cash. Liabilities are what the company owes to others, such as loans or accounts payable. Equity represents the residual interest in the assets of the company after deducting liabilities.

Ask Notion Who Is The Best At ...

Notion AI not only knows the answers to subject-related questions, but it can also suggest who the best expert is in a given topic and the main thesis of their work.

Use the prompt: Give me a list of the most famous expert in...

Input to Notion AI:

Give me a list of the most famous expert in management

Output from Notion AI:

Most famous experts in management

- Peter Drucker
- Stephen Covey
- Ken Blanchard
- John Kotter
- Gary Hamel

After that, ask about the books written by each author with a prompt List of the best books of ...author name...

Example of Output from Notion about the books from Peter Drucker:

- *The Effective Executive*
- *Management Challenges for the 21st Century*
- *Innovation and Entrepreneurship: Practice and Principles*
- *The Practice of Management*
- *The Essential Drucker*

Ask AI to give you an outline with key ideas of the books with a prompt Create an outline of the book ... Authors - Name of the book...

Example of Notion AI output key ideas outline of the book *Peter Drucker - The Effective Executive*

1. Introduction
   - Explanation of the importance of effective executives in organizations
2. The Executive
   - Definition of an executive
   - The executive's role in the organization
3. Effectiveness
   - The difference between efficiency and effectiveness
   - The importance of focusing on effectiveness
4. Time Management
   - Techniques for managing time effectively
   - Importance of prioritizing tasks
5. Decision Making
   - The decision-making process
   - Techniques for making effective decisions
6. Communication
   - Importance of effective communication in organizations
   - Techniques for improving communication skills
7. Leadership
   - The qualities of effective leaders

- Techniques for developing leadership skills

8. Conclusion
   - Summary of key points
   - Importance of effective executives for organizational success

Ask to explain more detail about any part of the outline you are interested in.

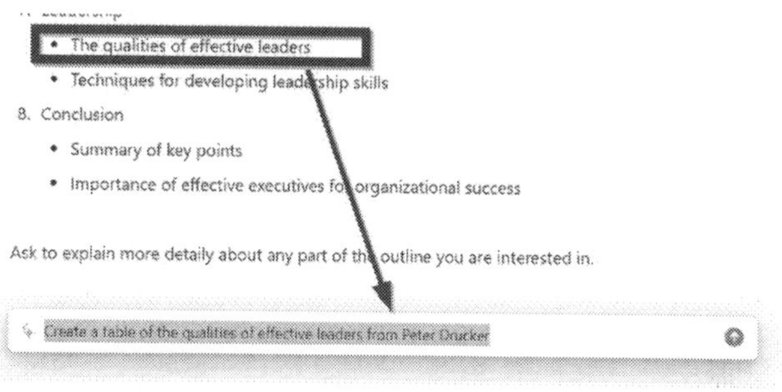

Notion AI output about qualities of an effective leader from Peter Drucker's book The Effective Executive:

Quality	Description
Clear vision and goals	Effective leaders have a clear idea of what they want to achieve and can articulate that vision to others. They set clear goals and objectives and work towards achieving them.
Strong communication skills	Effective leaders are able to communicate clearly and effectively with their team members. They listen actively, provide feedback, and foster open communication.
Ability to inspire and motivate others	Effective leaders are able to inspire and motivate their team members to perform at their best. They lead by example and create a positive work environment.
Ability to make decisions	Effective leaders are decisive and able to make difficult decisions when necessary. They analyze information and weigh the pros and cons before making a decision.
Willingness to take risks	Effective leaders are willing to take calculated risks in order to achieve their goals. They are not afraid to try new things and are willing to learn from their failures.
Strong problem-solving skills	Effective leaders are able to identify problems and find solutions quickly and efficiently. They are creative and resourceful in their approach to problem-solving.
Ability to delegate tasks	Effective leaders are able to delegate tasks to their team members and trust them to complete those tasks. They provide guidance and support as needed.
Empathy and emotional intelligence	Effective leaders are able to understand and empathize with their team members. They are able to connect with others on an emotional level and create a supportive work environment.
Strong work ethic	Effective leaders lead by example and work hard to achieve their goals. They are committed to their work and are willing to put in the time and effort required to succeed.
Focus on continuous learning and development	Effective leaders are always looking for ways to improve themselves and their team members. They seek out new challenges and opportunities for growth and encourage their team members to do the same.

Create Summaries From Your Booking Notes

Use Notion AI to create summary, extract the main ideas from the books you read use - /summarize block for it

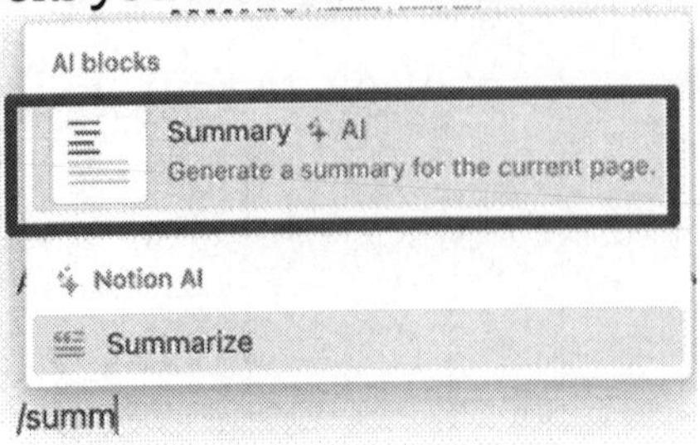

Here how looks like summarize block

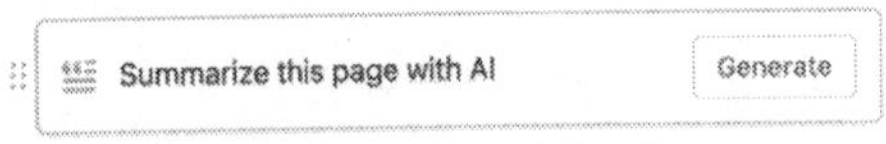

Notion AI summary block

Embed this block to the Book Notes template page to get summaries of each book you read in 1 click!Pocket,

With the online tool https://readwise.io/ you can synchronize your book notes from Kindle, Instapaper, iBooks with Notion.

Solving Math Problems

Ask Notion for help with math problems. But you need to be careful because sometimes Notion makes mistakes in calculations; that's why it is better to ask for step-by-step calculations.

Example of Notion AI input:

What is the surface area of a sphere with a radius 10. Let's think in steps and format the answer as a list.

Example of Notion AI output:

1. The formula for the surface area of a sphere is $4\pi r^2$.
2. Substitute the value of the radius into the formula: $4\pi(10)^2$.
3. Simplify the expression: $4\pi(100) = 400\pi$.
4. The surface area of the sphere is approximately 1256.64 square units.

Write An Essay

Ask Notion AI to generate an essay with the command /Essay - just start typing it and you'll see the menu below

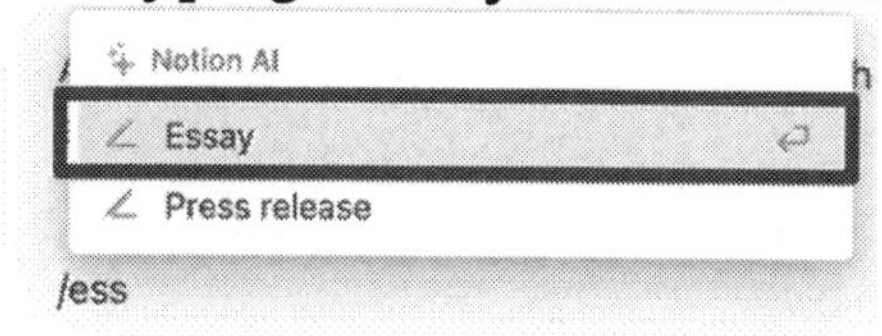

Enter topic you want to write about

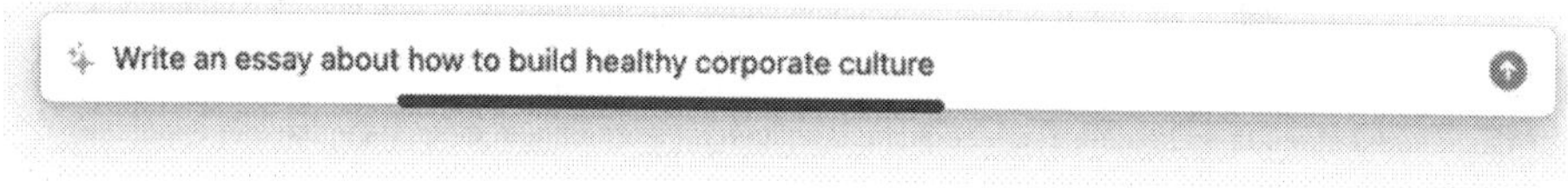

Notion AI output is below:

Building a Healthy Corporate Culture

A healthy corporate culture is essential for any organization that wants to thrive in today's highly competitive business world. It is the foundation upon which the company is built, and it determines how employees interact with each other, how they interact with customers, and how they feel about their work.

In this essay, we will discuss the key components of building a healthy corporate culture.

Importance of a Healthy Corporate Culture

A healthy corporate culture is vital for the success of any organization. It creates an environment where employees feel valued, respected, and motivated to perform at their best. It also fosters teamwork, collaboration, and innovation, which are critical for achieving business objectives. In addition, a healthy corporate culture can help attract and retain top talent, as employees are more likely to stay with a company that values and invests in their well-being.

Key Components of a Healthy Corporate Culture

1.Clear Mission, Vision, and Values

A clear mission, vision, and values statement is the foundation of a healthy corporate culture. It provides a sense of direction and purpose to the organization and helps employees understand what the company stands for. A well-defined mission, vision, and values statement also helps create a sense of unity among employees and provides a framework for decision-making.

2.Strong Leadership

Strong leadership is another critical component of a healthy corporate culture. Leaders set the tone for the organization and influence the behavior and attitudes of employees. Effective leaders inspire and motivate employees, promote a positive work environment, and lead by example. They also communicate effectively, provide feedback, and create opportunities for growth and development.

3.Open Communication

Open communication is essential for building a healthy corporate culture. When employees feel free to express their opinions and ideas, it fosters a sense of trust and respect among team members. It also promotes transparency and helps ensure that everyone is working towards the same goals. To encourage open communication, companies should provide channels for feedback, hold regular team meetings, and provide opportunities for employees to collaborate on projects.

4.Employee Well-being

Employee well-being is a critical aspect of a healthy corporate culture. When employees feel supported and valued, they are more likely to be engaged and productive. Companies can promote employee well-being by providing opportunities for work-life balance, offering health and wellness programs, and providing resources for mental health support.

Conclusion

In conclusion, building a healthy corporate culture is essential for any organization that wants to succeed in today's business world. It requires a clear mission, vision, and values statement, strong leadership, open communication, and a focus on employee well-being. By investing in these key components, companies can create a positive work environment that fosters teamwork, collaboration, and innovation, ultimately leading to greater success and profitability.

If you need to expand some parts - highlight it and ask - continue writing

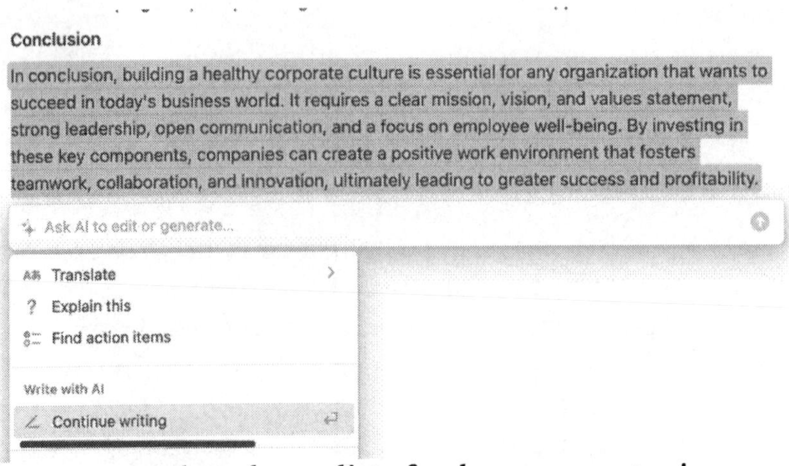

Also, you can ask to show a list of web-pages on a topic you want to research with the command: Create a bulleted list of web-pages on this topic and press Enter

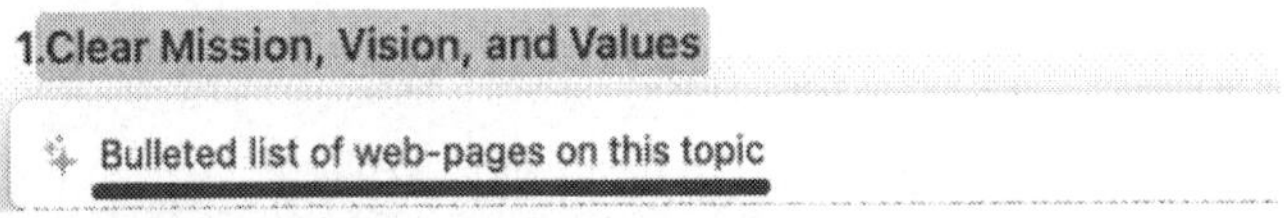

Here is an output from Notion AI:

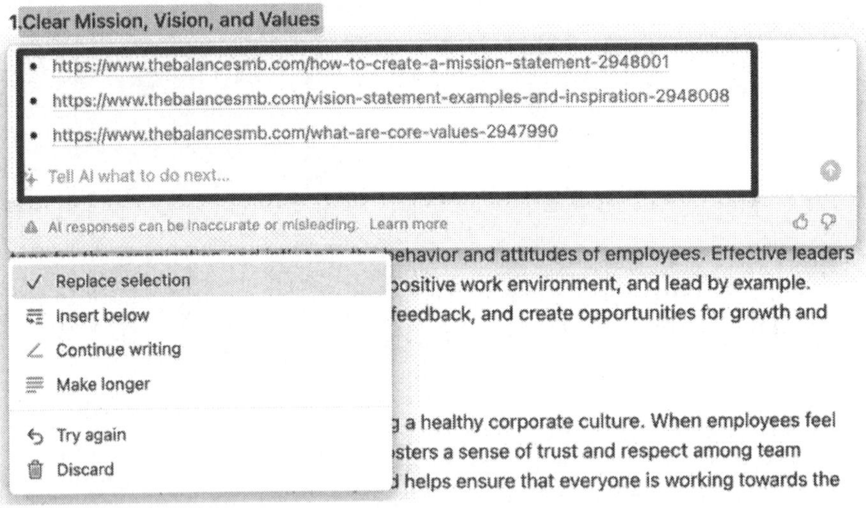

Also you can ask Notion AI to create a table with books or authors that write on topics you are interested in.

Just highlight the ideas in which you are interested and use this

prompt in Notion AI:

Give a list any authors, books or notable sources that write about this term and contextualise each one in a table and press Enter

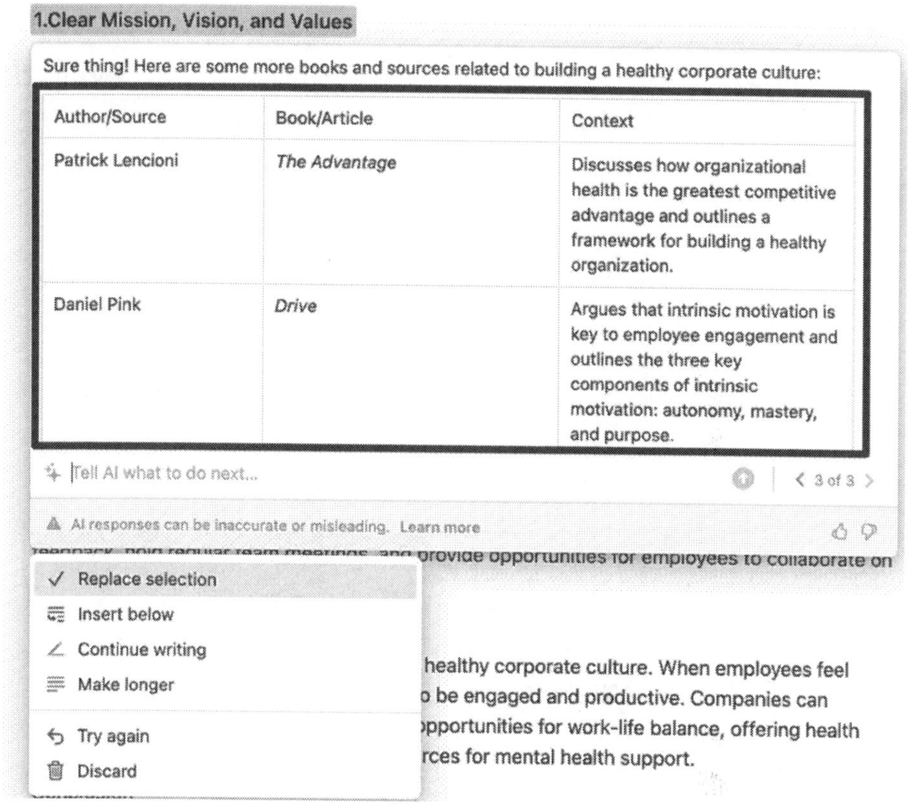

Ask To Test You Knowledge About Essay Wrote By Notion Ai

Prepare to answer questions about the essay you wrote with Notion AI, and here are some sample questions to help you prepare:

Write me 10 questions to test myself on the above material and press Enter

Input to Notion AI:

members. It also promotes transparency and helps ensure that everyone is working towards the same goals. To encourage open communication, companies should provide channels for feedback, hold regular team meetings, and provide opportunities for employees to collaborate on projects.

4.Employee Well-being

Employee well-being is a critical aspect of a healthy corporate culture. When employees feel supported and valued, they are more likely to be engaged and productive. Companies can promote employee well-being by providing opportunities for work-life balance, offering health and wellness programs, and providing resources for mental health support.

Conclusion

In conclusion, building a healthy corporate culture is essential for any organization that wants to succeed in today's business world. It requires a clear mission, vision, and values statement, strong leadership, open communication, and a focus on employee well-being. By investing in these key components, companies can create a positive work environment that fosters teamwork, collaboration, and innovation, ultimately leading to greater success and profitability.

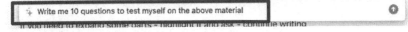

Write me 10 questions to test myself on the above material

Notion AI output:

1. What are the four key components of a healthy corporate culture?
2. Why is a clear mission, vision, and values statement important for a healthy corporate culture?
3. What is the role of strong leadership in building a healthy corporate culture?
4. How can open communication foster a healthy corporate culture?
5. Why is employee well-being critical for a healthy corporate culture?
6. What are some ways companies can promote employee well-being?
7. How can a healthy corporate culture benefit an organization?
8. What are some potential drawbacks of an unhealthy corporate culture?
9. How can companies create a positive work environment that fosters teamwork and collaboration?
10. What is the ultimate goal of investing in key

components that create a healthy corporate culture?

If you want to get questions answered, correct your prompt to:

Write me 10 questions and answers to test myself on the above material

Notion AI output:

1. What are the four key components of a healthy corporate culture?
    - Clear mission, vision, and values
    - Strong leadership
    - Open communication
    - Employee well-being
2. How does a clear mission, vision, and values statement contribute to a healthy corporate culture?
    - It provides a sense of direction and purpose to the organization and helps employees understand what the company stands for.
3. What is the role of strong leadership in building a healthy corporate culture?
    - Leaders set the tone for the organization and influence the behavior and attitudes of employees. Effective leaders inspire and motivate employees, promote a positive work environment, and lead by example.
4. What is the importance of open communication in building a healthy corporate culture?
    - Open communication fosters a sense of trust and respect among team members, promotes transparency, and helps ensure that everyone is working towards the same goals.
5. How can companies promote employee well-being in order to achieve a healthy corporate culture?
    - They can provide opportunities for work-life balance, offer health and wellness programs, and provide resources for mental health support.
6. Why is employee well-being critical for a healthy

corporate culture?

- When employees feel supported and valued, they are more likely to be engaged and productive.

7. What are some potential drawbacks of an unhealthy corporate culture?
   - Low employee morale, low productivity, high turnover rates, and a negative impact on the company's reputation.
8. How can companies create a positive work environment that fosters teamwork and collaboration?
   - By encouraging open communication, providing opportunities for feedback, and creating opportunities for employees to collaborate on projects.
9. What is the ultimate goal of investing in key components that create a healthy corporate culture?
   - To create a positive work environment that fosters teamwork, collaboration, and innovation, ultimately leading to greater success and profitability.
10. How can a healthy corporate culture benefit an organization?
    - It creates an environment where employees feel valued, respected, and motivated to perform their best. It also fosters teamwork, collaboration, and innovation, which are critical for achieving business objectives. In addition, a healthy corporate culture can help attract and retain top talent, as employees are more likely to stay with a company that values and invests in their well-being.

CHAPTER 4. TIPS & TRICKS WITH NOTION AI

Dark mode in Notion

If you prefer working with a dark screen, you can easily switch to Dark Mode in Notion. To do this, go to the Settings & Members menu → My notifications & settings → and finally, Appearance or use hotkeys CTRL + SHIFT + L (for mac: CMD + SHIFT + L)

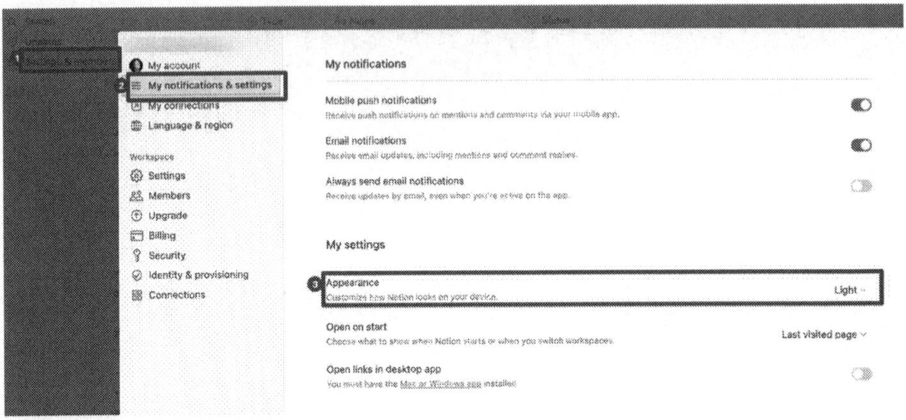

Use AI summaries with table of content

Place the AI Summary block in the second column opposite the table of content and generate the summary in one click. This is convenient for meetings, book outlines, articles, etc.

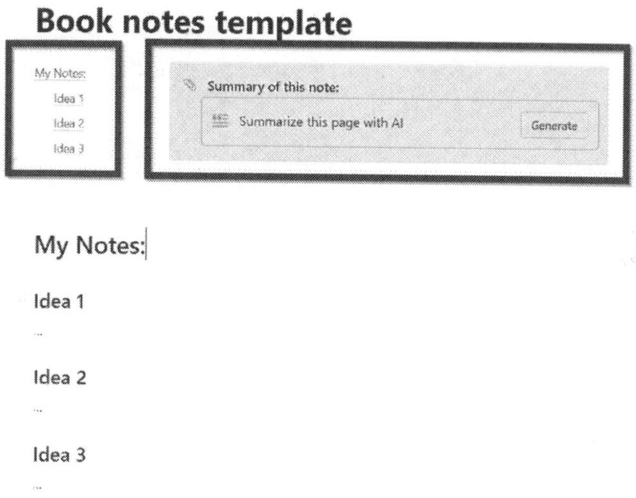

Turn tables generated by AI into databases

Convert the comparative table generated by Notion AI into a database in one click. It helps to dive deeply into each point and write each one on a new page.

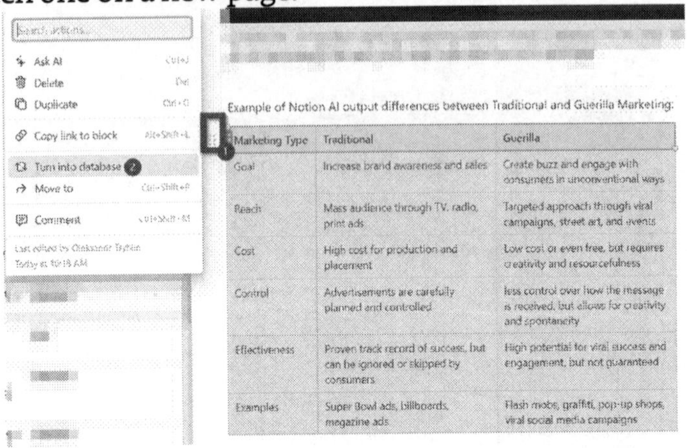

Example of database that we got after conversion from comparison table

Comparison table +

Filter Sort New

Traditional vs Guerilla Marketing

Aa Marketing Type	Traditional	Guerilla
Goal	Increase brand awareness and sales	Create buzz and engage with consumers in unconventional ways
Reach	Mass audience through TV, radio, print ads	Targeted approach through viral campaigns, street art, and events
Cost	High cost for production and placement	Low cost or even free, but requires creativity and resourcefulness
Control	Advertisements are carefully planned and controlled	less control over how the message is received, but allows for creativity and spontaneity
Effectiveness	Proven track record of success, but can be ignored or skipped by consumers	High potential for viral success and engagement, but not guaranteed
Examples	Super Bowl ads, billboards, magazine ads	Flash mobs, graffiti, pop-up shops, viral social media campaigns

+ New

Calculate

Locate pros and cons in 2 columns

Ask Notion AI to write a list of pros and cons for any topic you want, and after that, place these paragraphs in two columns opposite each other, it will be much more convenient to read them.

The following is an example of a pros and cons Notion AI:

Pros

- Notion AI can save you time by automating certain tasks.
- It can help with organizing your notes and tasks by suggesting tags and categories.
- The AI-powered search feature makes it easier to find specific information within your Notion workspace.
- With machine learning, Notion AI can learn from your behavior and adapt to your needs.
- Notion AI can assist with natural language processing to make text input easier.

Cons

- Notion AI is not yet perfect and can sometimes make mistakes or suggest irrelevant tags.
- The AI-powered features are limited to certain aspects of the Notion app and may not be applicable to all users.
- Some users may feel uncomfortable with AI having access to their personal information and data.
- Notion AI is not a replacement for human interaction and collaboration.
- The AI-powered features may not be as customizable as some users would prefer.

Drag and drop text in the 2nd column:

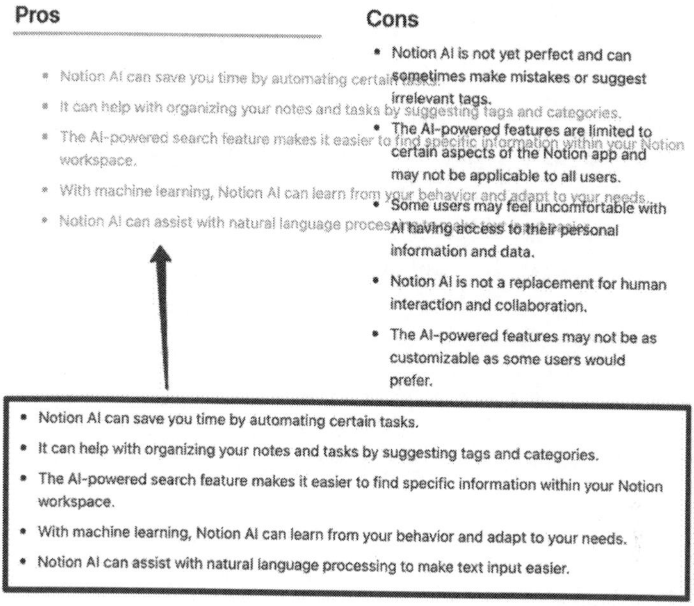
Pros
Cons
Notion AI is not yet perfect and can sometimes make mistakes or suggest irrelevant tags.
The AI-powered features are limited to certain aspects of the Notion app and may not be applicable to all users.
Some users may feel uncomfortable with AI having access to their personal information and data.
Notion AI is not a replacement for human interaction and collaboration.
The AI-powered features may not be as customizable as some users would prefer.
Notion AI can save you time by automating certain tasks.
It can help with organizing your notes and tasks by suggesting tags and categories.
The AI-powered search feature makes it easier to find specific information within your Notion workspace.
With machine learning, Notion AI can learn from your behavior and adapt to your needs.
Notion AI can assist with natural language processing to make text input easier.

Specify the number of characters you want to see the text size

For example, if we have an intro text about Notion AI and we want to make it longer for 2000 symbols for an Instagram post, highlight the text and use the command Make this text 2000 characters long and press Enter

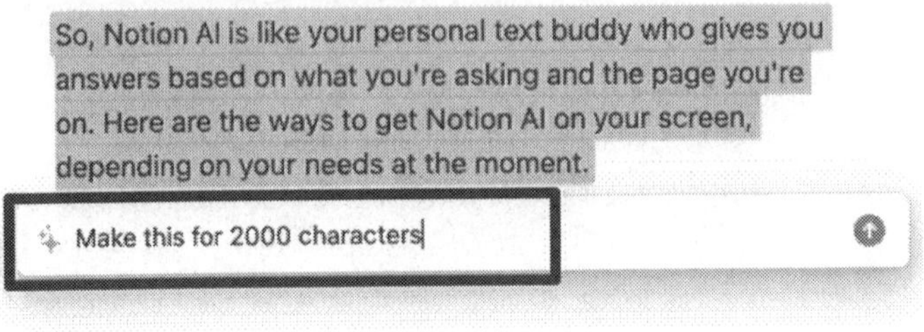
So, Notion AI is like your personal text buddy who gives you answers based on what you're asking and the page you're on. Here are the ways to get Notion AI on your screen, depending on your needs at the moment.
Make this for 2000 characters

Example of output:

So, Notion AI is like your personal text buddy who gives you answers based on what you're asking and the page you're on. Here are the ways to get Notion AI on your screen, depending on your needs at the moment. If you're looking to streamline your workflow and make your life easier, Notion AI is the perfect tool for you. It's like having a personal assistant at your fingertips, ready to help you with anything you need. Whether you're looking for answers to specific questions, want to automate tasks, or just need a little help staying organized, Notion AI has got you covered. Simply type in your query and let the AI do the rest. With Notion AI, you can save time and focus on what's important – getting things done. So why wait? Try Notion AI today and see how it can transform the way you work!

Integrate Save to Notion widget and Notion AI to get summaries of articles

Use Save to Notion widget for Chrome to save articles from Web

https://chrome.google.com/webstore/detail/save-to-notion/ldmmifpegigmeammaeckplhnjbbpccmm?hl=en

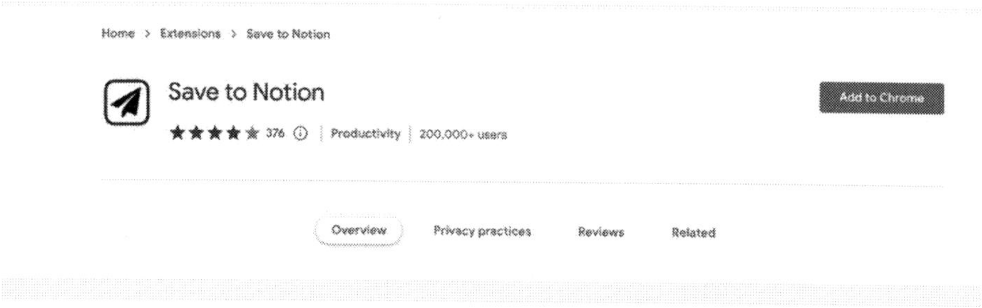

And Notion AI can write summaries for the saved articles using the /summarize block

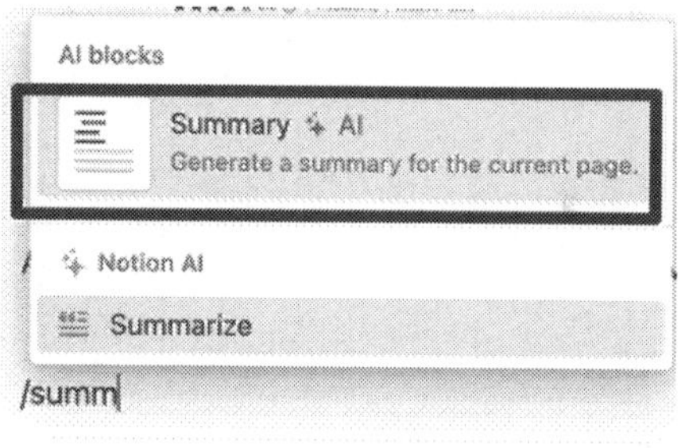

Here's how the summarized block looks (you can embed it in your Notion template page):

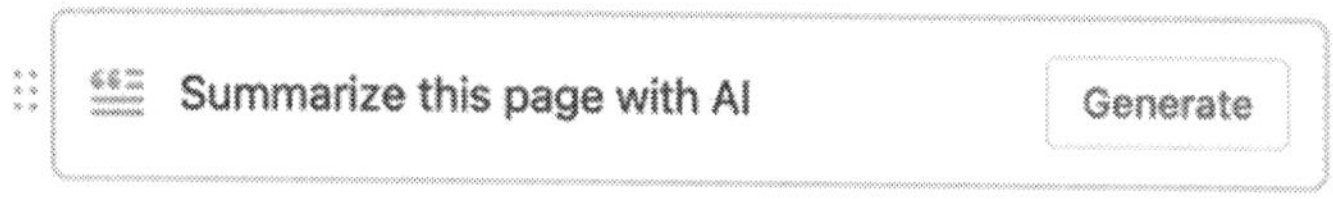

Example of summary input of this page

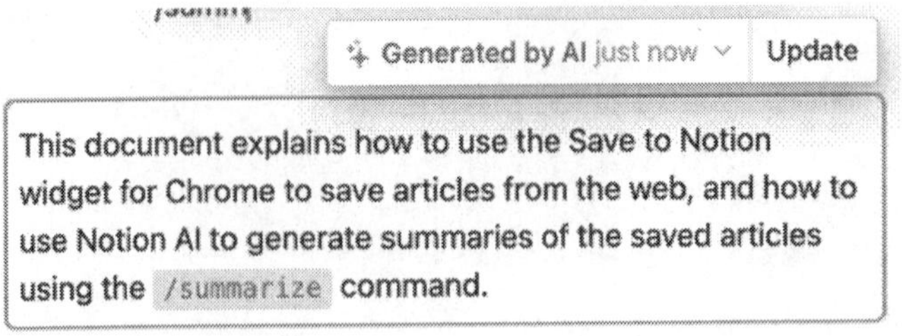
Generated by AI just now
Update
This document explains how to use the Save to Notion widget for Chrome to save articles from the web, and how to use Notion AI to generate summaries of the saved articles using the /summarize command.

Create page with favorite prompts

Create a page where you will save interesting prompts and use them regularly

Examples:

- Convert oz to kg

  Convert **10** oz to kg

- Convert ft to cm

  Convert **6 ft 2 inches** to cm

- Convert hours to decimals

  Convert **1h 20 min** to decimals

- Make this text 2000 characters long

CHAPTER 5. PROS AND CONS NOTION AI

Advantages of Notion AI

All In One Place

Notion AI integrating artificial intelligence into the place where you work. So you won't have to constantly switch between separate AI-powered tools. Keep up the great work in one window!

Unique And Flexible Text Editor With Blocks

Notion's drag-and-drop text editor is really cool and unique compared to other tools out there. It's also super flexible, so you can easily rearrange and transform any AI-generated content with ease. Plus, over time, Notion AI will be able to take advantage of even more of Notion's awesome features, like using databases for AI prompts.

Templates With Integrated Notion Ai Buttons

Notion prepared a list of 9 templates with Notion AI, that will improve your productivity - enjoy it:

1. Product Launch Announcement (w/ Notion AI)

https://www.notion.so/templates/product-launch-announcement-w-notion-ai

2. Feature FAQs (w/ Notion AI)

https://www.notion.so/templates/feature-faqs-w-notion-ai

3. Plan a Trip (w/ Notion AI)

https://www.notion.so/templates/plan-a-trip-w-notion-ai

4. Sales Outreach (w/ Notion AI)

https://www.notion.so/templates/sales-outreach-w-notion-ai

5. Weekly Meal Prep (w/ Notion AI)

https://www.notion.so/templates/weekly-meal-prep-w-notion-ai

6. Job Descriptions (w/ Notion AI)

https://www.notion.so/templates/job-descriptions-w-notion-ai

7. Meeting Summaries (w/ Notion AI)

https://www.notion.so/templates/meeting-summaries-w-notion-ai

8. Product Localization (w/ Notion AI)

https://www.notion.so/templates/product-localization-w-notion-ai

9. Recruiting Outreach (w/ Notion AI)

https://www.notion.so/templates/recruiting-outreach-w-notion-ai

It's a good idea to create your favorite list with such a template and use it every day for all areas of your life.

Ready-Made Prompts

Notion analyzed popular requests and turned them into AI prompts, which is incredibly convenient. Instead of coming up with your own ideas, you can use what's already available.

Another point to note is that using AI to improve your writing can become a habit. Before, I would only edit my posts to correct errors. However, since discovering the "Improve writing" feature, I find myself using it constantly. It's pretty cool, actually.

Talk To Notion Ai In Native App For Ios/Android

Notion has a mobile app for iOS and Android, and it's very

convenient to use a smartphone or tablet to communicate with AI in the native Notion application.

Fixed Fee

Unlike OpenAI, where you pay for the number of words generated by AI (OpenAI pricing: https://openai.com/pricing), in Notion AI you pay a fixed amount of $10 per team member. A 20% discount is available to Plus, Business, and Enterprise customers with annual billing.

However, Notion AI reserves the right to reduce the number of requests you send if you make too many requests to Notion AI:

To ensure optimal performance and fair use across all Notion AI users, your access to AI features can be reduced depending on your usage.

Source: https://www.notion.so/help/ai-pricing-and-usage

Creating Comparison Tables

Asking Notion AI to compare something in a table view will generate a comparison analysis table. To activate it, type **/AI** to view AI blocks or press Space on the blank row, and ask Notion AI to Create a comparison table of ...

Below is example of comparison table created by Notion AI, about **volleyball** and **beach volleyball,** where prompt was Create a comparison table volleyball and beach volleyball (1) and below prompt you see the output from Notion AI (2) - it creating this table and filling it in real time

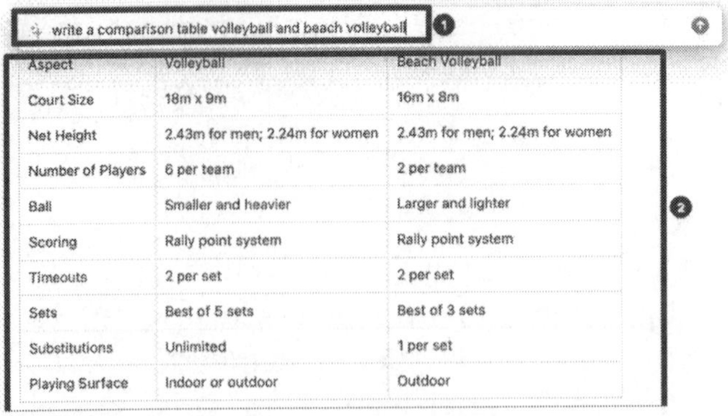

Aspect	Volleyball	Beach Volleyball
Court Size	18m x 9m	16m x 8m
Net Height	2.43m for men; 2.24m for women	2.43m for men; 2.24m for women
Number of Players	6 per team	2 per team
Ball	Smaller and heavier	Larger and lighter
Scoring	Rally point system	Rally point system
Timeouts	2 per set	2 per set
Sets	Best of 5 sets	Best of 3 sets
Substitutions	Unlimited	1 per set
Playing Surface	Indoor or outdoor	Outdoor

You can create a comparison table from your text as well; just select it and ask AI to create a comparison table.

Creating Actions Plan In One Click

During meetings, it's often necessary to quickly summarize and highlight next steps. Notion AI can handle this in just a few clicks

Just highlight the text with the meeting protocol and hit up Ask AI. Then, you can choose the option Find action items from the drop-down menu.

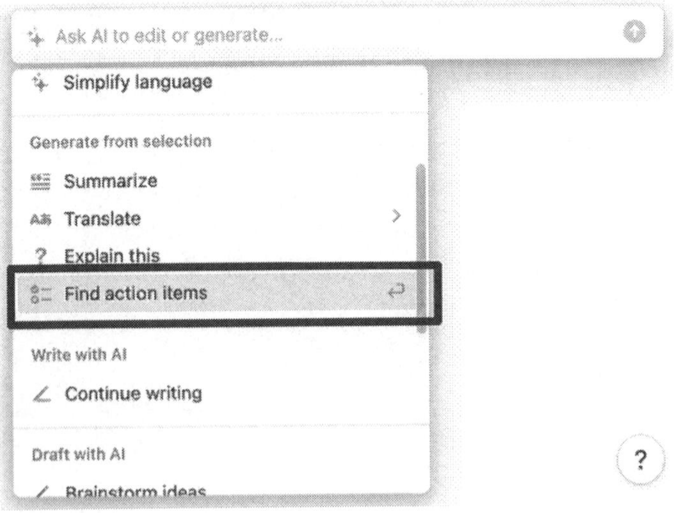

Keyboard Shortcuts That Speed Up Your Work

Working with Notion AI is very easy with the help of keyboard shortcuts.

Press the spacebar on a blank page, and a menu with Notion AI will appear.

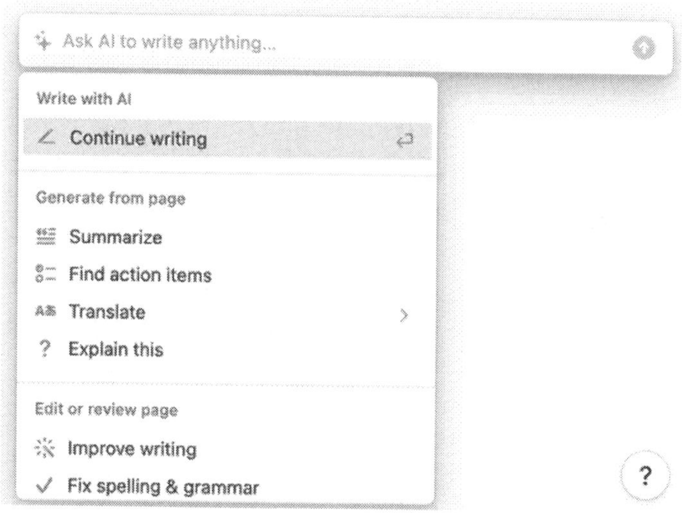

If you want to perform an action with text - select the text and press CTRL + J (on mac CMD + J)

Disadvantages of Notion AI

Notion Ai Can't Generate Images

Notion AI is a powerful tool for generating text, but it currently does not have the capability to generate images.

No Chat History With Ai

Unlike ChatGPT, where there is a chat history of communication with AI, Notion AI does not have such a history, and sometimes it would be nice to see the history of interaction with AI and the results it provided.

You Can't Purchase Notion Ai For Only Part Of Your Team

Notion AI can only be purchased for the entire workspace. Currently, there isn't an option to provision AI access to only a portion of your workspace.

Annual Customers Are Not Able To Purchase Notion Ai With Monthly Billing

Customers who opt for annual billing plans may find themselves limited to subscribing to Notion AI on a monthly basis, which can be a disadvantage for those who prefer more flexible payment options.

There Is No Access To Notion Ai For Guests

Guests will not be able to use AI features in a workspace that has a

Notion AI subscription.

Just 20 Free Trial Ai Responses

Notion AI offers only 20 free requests, which is very limited and often not enough to fully understand how it works and how it can help me in my business.

Notion AI competitors

- ChatGPT has a free plan available intermittently and a new $20/month unlimited plan.
- Canva Docs Magic Write is free for 25 uses on its free plan.
- Craft's AI assistant just doubled its offering to 100 uses on its free plan.
- Miro AI - generate ideas on a whiteboard, free AI output with some limitations

How does Notion position itself compared to competitors

Features	Notion AI	Grammarly Premium	ChatGPT Plus	Jasper
Monthly price (1 person)	$10	$12+	$20	$49+
Improve your writing	✓	✓	✓	✓
Write your first draft	✓		✓	✓
Access across all your notes, docs & projects	✓	✓		
Easy drag & drop text editor	✓			

Source: https://www.notion.so/product/ai

CONCLUSION

Notion AI is a sophisticated technology that uses natural language processing (like ChatGPT) to help users simplify tasks, automate workflows, and increase productivity. This tool is an excellent way to organize notes, databases, wikis, and more, making it an ideal solution for personal or professional use.

One of the key benefits of Notion AI is its ability to accurately interpret user input, making it possible to suggest and automate certain tasks. This allows users to create tables, format text, and link related pages quickly and efficiently, saving a significant amount of time and effort.

We hope you have learned a lot of interesting ideas from this book on how you can use Notion AI, even if you are not an active Notion user.

If you want to develop further and get more ideas on this topic, become a member of our "AI-Powered Business Solutions" community, where there will be more examples and cases from businesses on how to use AI tools to develop your business and team.

Apply for membership "AI-Powered Business Solutions" community for free here: aipbs.net

REFERENCE MATERIALS

Official Notion pages.

Notion official guide: learn how to use Notion AI to transform text, automate simple tasks, and generate new content inside your connected workspace.

https://www.notion.so/help/guides/notion-ai-for-docs

AI pricing & usage: Here's the deal with how much you can use Notion AI and how much it'll cost you. Basically, this is the lowdown on pricing and usage limits.

https://www.notion.so/help/ai-pricing-and-usage

Notion AI FAQs: Frequently asked questions about Notion AI

https://www.notion.so/help/notion-ai-faqs

Notion AI Supplementary Terms: These Notion AI Supplementary Terms are part of the Personal Use Terms of Service and the Master Subscription Agreement between the user and Notion. They apply to the user's access and use of any Notion AI feature(s) and, if applicable, the Notion AI Add-On Subscription

https://www.notion.so/Notion-AI-Supplementary-Terms-fa9034c8b5a04818a6baf3eac2adddbb

Master Subscription Agreement: The main document that describes the terms of the user agreement for the Notion subscription

https://www.notion.so/Master-Subscription-Agreement-4e1c5dd3e3de45dfa4a8ed60f1a43da0

Service Level Terms: This document outlines the availability requirements for Notion's services, which must be available 99.9% of the time, excluding scheduled maintenance and downtime resulting from reasons beyond Notion's control. Also here is mention what If Notion fails to meet this requirement.

https://www.notion.so/Service-Level-Terms-6f805fa1d4ca4463b805e2832ae8ff0d

YouTube videos that helped us prepare this book:

Adrian Twarog - Top 10 AI Tools Like ChatGPT You Must Try in 2023

https://www.youtube.com/watch?v=eLVQpTWxYys

Better Creating - Incredible Chat GPT & Notion AI Tips That WORK. All This In 1-Day?!

https://www.youtube.com/watch?v=9cMiH8eMyvM

Bri Builds - ChatGPT vs. Notion AI: Side-by-Side Prompt Comparisons

https://www.youtube.com/watch?v=2p-ezfaYCFA Bri Builds - 5 Amazing Ways I use Notion Ai to Save HOURS of Time

https://www.youtube.com/watch?v=bbnKz9KH3Yc Kharma Medic - Notion AI is AMAZING - How to use Notion AI: Tutorial & Examples

https://www.youtube.com/watch?v=sBkYPri_-vU

Notion - Introducing Notion AI

https://www.youtube.com/watch?v=FElBbgnNtVA

Notion - Notion AI is here, for everyone

https://www.youtube.com/watch?v=RDZ3mY10zY8

Oliur - Notion AI - How to use it and get the most out of it

https://www.youtube.com/watch?v=L_jWvpN2VlE

Productive Dude - Notion AI: Full Guide for Beginners (2023 Notion AI Tutorial)

https://www.youtube.com/watch?v=l_O_9wAhjio

Red Gregory - NEW! Notion AI: Everything You Need to Know (32 min)

https://www.youtube.com/watch?v=6cnQveexDyw

Thomas Frank - NOTION AI IS HERE – 10 Mind-Blowing Examples!

https://www.youtube.com/watch?v=0DIn0Ws9yTE

Printed in Great Britain
by Amazon

23496177R00075